D. B Wright

The Future of the United States

By Divine appointment and the doom of monarchy as predicted in Revelation

D. B Wright

The Future of the United States
By Divine appointment and the doom of monarchy as predicted in Revelation

ISBN/EAN: 9783743407190

Manufactured in Europe, USA, Canada, Australia, Japa

Cover: Foto ©ninafisch / pixelio.de

Manufactured and distributed by brebook publishing software (www.brebook.com)

D. B Wright

The Future of the United States

THE FUTURE

OF THE

UNITED STATES

BY

DIVINE APPOINTMENT

AND THE

DOOM OF MONARCHY,

AS

PREDICTED IN REVELATION.

BY REV. D. B. WRIGHT.

1887.
ELIJAH GAY, PUBLISHER.
LOS ANGELES, CAL.

DEDICATION.

WE dedicate this little volume to the working class of America. For—to them we owe the liberty we enjoy; they have stood by our country in every instance; they have raised the provisions to feed their brethren in the field; and at one and the same time fought her battles, tilled the soil, and are ever ready to bear their breasts to the bullets when her free institutions are in danger. God bless them, and forever give into *their* hand the country they so richly deserve.

THE AUTHOR.

Entered according to act of Congress in the year 1887 by D. B. WRIGHT in the office of the Librarian of Congress at Washington.

INTRODUCTION.

That either the monarchical form of government, or the Republican form, *must* become universal on earth, is a self-evident truth. We Americans see very readily that the free. Democratic, representative form of government, of which we are the great successful representative, must and will supplant all monarchy and become universal. And it begins to be seen and felt by the crowned heads of Europe and the more enlightened and thoughtful of their subjects. The Empress Eugenie. several years ago, ventured the prophecy that in fifty years there would not be a crowned head in Europe. And an event that is so readily sanctioned by reason, and is such a natural and unavoidable sequence of our rapidly advancing civilization, and, above all, is plainly taught of God in the predictions of prophecy, must and will be among the events of subsequent history, and cannot be very far distant. The history of the world is but the history of God's dealings with the nations, and prophecy is but the history of nations pre-written.

Now, we claim in this unassuming book that God has a grand and glorious future for our nation, one that will make the heart of every true citizen swell with patriotic joy, and cause all lovers of Bible democracy in every land to rejoice with us. And in accomplishing it God will not use the great things of the world, great in the estimation of men, or the wise things of men. "But God hath chosen the foolish things of the world to confound the wise; and God hath chosen the weak things of the world to confound the things which are mighty: and base things of the world, and things which are despised, hath God chosen; yea, and things which are not, to bring to nought things that are." (I. Cor., 1—27.)

INTRODUCTION.

We announce here in the beginning of our book that God intends to accomplish the great future of our nation through the instrumentality of the laboring classes.

God has always claimed the poor of this world as his own peculiar inheritance. When his Son was in the world it was not the learned, the rich, and the great, or the officials in either church or state that received him, but the "common people heard him gladly."

This book claims that God's ancient nationality, the Jewish Republic in the wilderness, and finally established in the land of Canaan, was a type of which our nation is the antetype, he established that nation to prefigure our glorious nation in the "time of the end."

And when he established that nation he did not employ the wealth and power, and influence of kings and heroes and statesmen, etc., but he took a band of degraded, ignorant slaves, laboring in a brick yard in Egypt under task-masters; none could be found poorer, or weaker, or in a more hopeless condition, and the first dash he made with them he shook proud Pharoah's throne to the dust, and nearly destroyed the most powerful empire in the world.

God uses only those things that are put in his hands freely and voluntarily to be used according to his will. Those possessed of wealth or power of any kind will not do this, but the poor of all ages have ever lifted their hands to heaven and prayed: "Our Father lead us."

God intended in raising up this nation to establish a nation in which the elective franchise should be in the hands of the laboring classes, and that the masses should rule, and not a hereditary aristocracy as in Europe, nor an aristocracy built upon a monied monopoly as in America, for it is a well known fact that in our glorious "land of the free," a monied monopoly seeks to throttle our government, and we call upon the working men of America to wield that mighty weapon which God has placed in our fingers—THE BALLOT—take to yourselves that mighty power, and rule this nation as God has intended you should.

We asked an ex-senator not long since what would be the end of this monied monopoly that was so rapidly gathering strength in our nation, and he replied, that it was the opinion of most men that it would end in the destruction of life and property. Well, now there is no need of that; if you will take to yourselves your right and your power to rule this nation before it is rested from you. No people have a right to resort to severe means while they hold in their grasp the elective franchise; when that is rested from them, then death to tyrants in any form is justifiable; that is why we sympathize with the poor people of Russia who are writhing beneath the iron heel of despotism. They have not the omnipotent ballot or if they have any power in that direction it is very suspiciously and vigilantly guarded, and neutralized by the few that, in Russia, seem determined cost what it will, to rule the many; that magnanimous *few* that ever seeks to rule the many have always been found in every age and in all lands, even in our beloved America.

Now, my countrymen, suffer this little hortatory as an introduction to our book, and put your ballot where it will tell for you and your children; where it will tell for liberty of the press, freedom of speech, and freedom of conscience.

We shall now address ourselves to the task of showing God's hand in our rise, growth, and glorious future that awaits us, and also His direct interposition in the overthrow and utter annihilation of monarchy on the earth.

PREFACE.

We do not claim to be a discoverer. The honor of the discovery of the following theory is, we think, due to the late Dr. Baldwin. We give his views in his own language, or nearly so, but we do not follow him strictly in our own views. We take him only in the main features. While we readily acknowledge that without him we could not see as far as he did, as we are privileged to stand upon his shoulders, we ought to see farther. We take up this GREAT subject because those who rank among the scholars of our day, hence have the power of research necessary to the great task, and ought to take it up and give the ministry as well as the laity some definite theory of prophecy, refuse to do so.

But they might reply to my friendly censure by telling me that I can afford to "tackle" it, as I have all to gain and nothing to lose, while they have all to lose and nothing to gain.

But we are encouraged in this bold adventure, feeling the blessing of God upon us in it, and emboldened by the fact that that time promised to Daniel when the Prophecies should be unsealed, has come, "the time of the end," not end of time, as some read; that would have been useless to have given to the world of mankind a revelation that was not intended to be understood until it was too late for mankind to be profited by it. Such a thought is too dishonoring to God. Nay, leave it to the heathen oracles to surround themselves with an imaginary mystery, well suited to awe the marvelousness of human nature. But God says His revelation was sent as a light into the world, and "that no prophecy of the Scriptures is of any private interpretation, and is profitable for doctrine, for reproof, for correction, for *instruction* in righteousness." A prophecy given in one dispensation of time, to transpire during a future period or dispensation of time, is sometimes sealed, or intentionally hidden from us, until the beginning of that period, when it becomes the duty of all God's enlightened people to discern them, and even the unconverted world that lieth in darkness is held culpable for not recognizing God's hand in the unfolding events.

While God gives the Prophecies in such occult language as to not be understood until they begin to be fulfilled, or, in other words, until they are unsealed, he does hold us culpable for not discerning them when that time arrives. One of the most severe rebukes which Christ dealt to the people of his day was for their not discerning the fulfillment of the Prophecies, then being fulfilled before their eyes.

We claim for the following theory that it systematizes the Prophecies. It will be readily discerned by the Bible student that the true theory would of necessity throw all prophecy into a beautiful and harmonious system, and that no other theory could, hence the leading principle to be laid down, in the interpretation of prophecy, is that it must systematize and harmonize the Prophets. . Error cannot be systematized; truth only can. All interpretations must coincide with the literal and evangelical doctrines of the Bible. It is a true maxim that "the perfect coincidence of events with prophecy is infallible proof of the fulfillment of prophecy." Jesus held closely to this principle, strictly fulfilling all that the prophets had predicted of Him, and it is in recognition of this principle that we believe in Him as the true Messiah.

Many predictions refer to two, and sometimes more, events, as in the case of Matt· ii., 17, 18. If we look at Jer. xxxi. 15, we will find those words applied to altogether another and different event, as Dr. Adam Clark plainly shows; also see Adam Clark on Isaiah, lxi. 1, where he shows the double application more forcibly as Jesus makes the application himself. It is a peculiarity of prophecy to give "here a little and there a little," hence one sentence will follow another, as wide apart in their application as the first and second advent of Christ. As in Luke iv. 18, there our blessed Saviour "went into the synagogue on the Sabbath day and stood up to read," and he read from the book of the Prophet Isaiah, and he stopped reading in the middle of a sentence. Now, it is evident to our mind that the omitted part of the sentence applies to his second coming to our world. He closed the book and sat down, and said unto them: "This day is this Scripture fulfilled in your ears." When He comes again will He not finish the sentence with propriety?

THE UNITED STATES IN THE RESTORATION.

All the intellectual creatures of God throughout the universe have a dual nature; a spiritual nature that constitutes them religious beings, and a social nature that constitutes them political beings; hence God's great universal empire is in keeping with these two principles, and is of a dual nature. These two constitutional qualities in man "have resulted universally in some kind of religion and some kind of civil government. In a state of purity and perfection, as with the angels in Heaven, or with man as he was first created, this has resulted in a pure religion and a perfect civil government. At the fall of man, the rejection of the true God as monarch in both of these departments, led to the wildest disorder and universal misery. Probably the greatest corruption visible to mortals is brought to view in human governments.

A great mind has said: "It is a truth, established by universal experience, that all civil governments among mankind have conformed in principle and practice to the genius of the prevailing religion of the people." Religion has controlled the politics of the world in all ages. If the religion has been mild so has been the civil government; if it has been bloody and despotic, so has been the civil government; if it has been liberal and enlightened, so has been the civil policy. This has resulted from a law of nature, by which inferior things are controlled by superior; and as the spiritual nature of man exercises supreme power over his conduct in his individual capacity, so does it in his aggregated state. To subdue man it was, therefore, necessary to subjugate his spiritual nature first, to regenerate him as a religious race, and then his political regeneration would follow inevitably. A physical victory might have resulted in a moment from the weight of Omnipotence, but a moral victory could not thus speedily be obtained from the eternal and immutable and self-existent principle of moral agency. As it is the natural result of all kinds of religion to form its subjects into some kind of civil government, so it has been with the religion of the Bible.

The Jewish Church, as soon as it extricated itself from bondage, formed itself into a nationality. That nationality, on account of the backsliding and infidelity of the people, came to an end, as it had been predicted by their prophets. At the same time they predicted its rise again and establishment on earth as the Israel of God to endure forever. There is nothing more forcibly predicted in the word of inspiration than the restoration of Israel. All the prophets have dwelt upon it and spoke of its future glory in the most extravagant language, and use the loftiest types and symbols, from Daniel to St. John, the Apocalypse, and the Christian world has ever looked and is still looking for its rise. Now, Israel restored is to be a nationality naturally arising out of God's recognized Church. The Christian Church claims to be that Church. We have come in the place of the Jewish Church. As the Apostle Paul says: "The Jews being the natural vine, and being broken off through unbelief, we gentiles, a wild olive tree, are grafted onto the natural stock." But he says also: "There is no difference between Jew and Gentile; we are all counted in unbelief and are all received through faith, whether Jew or Gentile, for he is not a Jew, which is one outwardly, neither is that circumcision which is outward in the flesh; but he is a Jew, which is one inwardly, and circumcision is that of the heart, in the spirit and not in the letter, whose praise is not of men but of God. So it is Chistian Israel or, in other words, Christ's Israel, that is to be restored, but the Jews are to be comprehended in it, for I truly believe our Hebrew brethren will yet come to see and believe that Jesus Christ was and is the true

Messiah which was promised by their Prophets, and they, through faith will be received of God the same as we Gentiles are received by faith, and they, coming with that true inward circumcision of the heart, they will bear a grand and glorious part in the glorious restoration of God's Israel.

But, in order to recognize God's Israel when it is restored and appears among the nations of the earth, we must know what kind of a nationality it will be, what kind of a government it will have. You will all see at a glance that there never was and never can be but two kinds of government. According to the constitution of man, there *can be but two* kinds of civil or spiritual government. All governments must either be republics or monarchies. There may be various kinds of each, but there is no harmonious medium kind, nor can there be. There may be absolute, limited, constitutional or hereditary monarchies, but they all agree in asserting or practicing the doctrine that the right of governing *does not* exist in the consent of the governed. There may be autocratic, democratic, representative and confederate republics, but they all agree there is no right of government except by the expressed consent of the governed. These two can never exist in a blended state harmoniously, because their principles are essentially and originally antagonistic. Now, it is equally plain that God's Israel, restored to nationality, must be a democratic republic.

First, because republican principles are the natural outgrowth of Christianity. Wherever Christianity is received into the human heart, and the man becomes imbued with its spirit, civil and religious liberty are at once felt to be the great blessings of man on earth. Again, nothing but a republic can be in keeping with the great law of love, as taught in the Gospel and throughout the Bible. "Thou shalt love the Lord thy God with all thy soul and strength and thy neighbor as thyself." This great law of God, the *dual law* of love supreme to God and equal love of neighbors, is justly called the great constitutional law of the universe, and the Decalogue, based upon it, is but the constitutional law of a single province of God's empire, as in our world. This great law of love to neighbor as to self, is a law conferring equal rights among all citizens of the same government. It is diametrically opposed to human legitimacy, p')acy, and absolutism. It is not conformable to hereditary a. .stocracy, nor can it be; it is democratic, purely, and places all citizens of the same country upon a dead level as to right to rule, and confers exclusive favors upon none. God is, according to it the only one that has a divine right to exercise kingship, and He is, by consequence, opposed to all human monarchy and hates it as a feature of hell. In the first book of Samuel, 8th chapter, we have the opinion of God and Israel about kings, and it is one of great repugnance on God's part and repentance on Israel's. Israel asked Samuel to make them a king, but he was displeased with the proposition and prayed to God about it, and God replied to him, "they have not rejected thee, but they have rejected me, that I should not reign over them. Now, therefore, hearken unto their voice, yet protest solemnly and shew them the manner of the king that shall reign over them." After a king was chosen, God signified his displeasure by a terrible thunder storm in wheat harvest, and the people were greatly terrified, for Samuel said, "I shall call unto the Lord, and He shall send thunder and rain that ye may perceive and see that your wickedness is great which ye have done in the sight of the Lord, in asking you a king," and the people said unto Samuel, "pray for thy servants unto the Lord thy God that we die not, for we have added unto all our sins this evil, to ask us a king."

It is evident that God considers a human monarchy as exceedingly sinful, and as standing in direct hostility to Himself, and he has but little patience with it. It is also obvious that in the recovery of the world to good government, in the progress of Christianity, that human monarchy will share no part nor lot in the new organization. God is, therefore, hostile to human monarchy, because the system is iniquitous in principle, and he will destroy it because of its wicked nature.

If you reply, "the powers that be are ordained of God," we answer that this does not prove monarchy correct in principle, for God uses monarchy as he does other *curses*, for the sake of chastising evil people. Thus the king of Babylon punished the Tyrians, and Cyrus punished Babylon at God's instigation, and wicked nations need tyrants to punish them for their vice. God said: "O, Israel, I will be thy king. I gave thee a king in my anger, and took him away in my wrath." Monarchy is, therefore, a curse added to a vicious people, who are unworthy of freedom. In the spiritual and political redemption of the world, it therefore follows that monarchy must be overthrown. God permits human monarchies to exist, and he always has a purpose in it, but all the governments He has established among men have been of the democratic-republican form. The government of the ancient Jews, their first government, the one God organized for them, was a theocratic democracy. Now, the Hebrew system was a typical one throughout, in both Church and State, and Israel restored to nationality, that nation which should arise in the world and endure forever, and should develop into the millennial kingdom, and to which we are told Christ is to come, is to be its ante-type.

All who read the Bible know that this nationality is unequivocally promised to Israel *in the Christian era, or latter day*. Now, the United States, being a late and extraordinary Christian people, arising late in the Christian era, we enquire may it not be the veritable nationality of the Prophets. If it coincides with all the great characteristics predicted of a Christian nationality, then all doubt must end, and our country, says Mr. Baldwin, "rise into an importance and sublimity absolutely overwhelming." And this is what we propose to show beyond a successful contradiction: We propose to show in these papers that this great nation is the one predicted by the Prophets, and is the great millennial kingdom in embryo.

We have said that the Hebrew Church and State were the type of which the Church and State, in the restoration of Israel to nationality, were to be the ante-type. About 300 years after the Jewish Church started in Abraham, it went into bondage in Egypt, and through Joseph was connected with the throne; and about 300 years after the Christian Church was established, it went into bondage by being connected with the throne of the Roman empire. As the Jewish Church came out of Egyptian bondage, crossed a sea and established a nationality in a wilderness, so the Christian Church came out of spiritual bondage in Europe, the Union of Church and State, and crossed a sea and established a nationality in a wilderness.

As many people in the American colonies were not pious, and yet approved of the liberty taught by Christianity, so many of the Hebrews were unbelievers in the religion of Moses, and yet approved and contended for the justness of constitutional liberty. Those who imagine that ante-typical Israel was to be composed of pure and holy men altogether, are *greatly* mistaken. On this principle, the Hebrew Church, as a type, would have required that every member of the ante-typical or Christian Church should have been holy. As the Church of typical Israel (Hebrew nation) possessed true doctrine, though many who belonged to it were impure, so the commonwealth of ante-typical Israel (Christianity in America) possesses the true doctrine of human government, though many who enjoy its benefits are not true Christians. Many Christians get a later period blended with the rise of Israel; they read that in the restoration all shall be taught of the Lord and all shall be holy, etc.; but if they would read a little more carefully, they would perceive that this is not said of the rise of Israel, it is of a later period.

In the end of time the angels shall gather out of the government of ante-typical Israel, or "out of the kingdom, all things that offend, and them that do iniquity."

As there were twelve tribes of Israel, and Joseph's tribe was divided, making thirteen, so William Penn had two colonies ceded to him, making just thirteen colonies in the restoration.*

'The Hebrew Confederacy was organized into a more perfect union after the exodus, by adopting a written democratic constitution, and so the Confederate colonies after the war of independence, in order to form a more perfect union, adopted a written, representative, democratic, federative constitution. The Hebrew constitution was submitted to the tribes for acceptance and ratification, and so was the American constitution. It is not a *little* remarkable that the Hebrew and American constitutions are the only two written ones ever known to have been adopted at the birth of any nationality prior to 1776.

The Hebrew bondage, consequent upon the descent into Egypt coincides with the civil and spiritual bondage suffered by spiritual Israel after the union of Church and State. The exodus from typical Egypt, the crossing a sea, the overthrow of Pharoah's host, the general thanksgiving, the organization of a republican confederacy of thirteen tribes, composed of three millions of people; the adoption of a written constitution by the tribes; the separation of the Church and State departments; their freedom from control of one by the other; their laws of servitude and naturalization, and their full organization and deliverance, under a noble leader in a wilderness, have all a complete correspondence in the United States of America.

We will take up now some of the literal prophecies of the

---

*Note Since these papers were written, we have seen in the public prints an account stating that they were about to bring the remains of William Penn to this country (ante-typical Israel) for interment. It would seem they were (without intending so to do) trying to make ante-typical Israel answer its type in detail. Joseph's bones had to be carefully 'aken up out of Egypt and buried in Israel.

restoration of Israel. And that we may better understand the literal prophecies, we will do well to keep before us the fact that God revealed to his Prophets, the *facts* but not always the *manner* of them. Again He did not increase their scientific knowledge; they spoke of everything in keeping with the scientific knowledge of their day.

The word of inspiration is so full of this class of prophecies, all so minutely pointing out our nation, that we hardly know where to begin. Perhaps it would be as well to commence with that prediction that so minutely describes the first settlement of this continent and the first inception of our nationality. This is recorded in Isaiah lx. 9: "Surely the isles shall wait for me and the ships of Tarshish, first to bring thy sons from far." To understand a prophecy, we must understand in what age of the world it was uttered, and where the prophet stood when he uttered it. This prophecy was made in Palestine in western Asia, called Asia Minor. There were vast countries at that day supposed to exist in the Atlantic, west of Gibraltar, and we are told by the best authority on history that they were termed "isles" by both Plato and Diodorus Siculus.

You will please observe that the Prophet represents God as speaking, and speaking in the first person, in the first part of the Prophecy, "the isles shall wait for *me*," and then he speaks in the second person, "and the ships of Tarshish, first to bring *thy* sons from far," as though he would say, "the great continent (lying on the other side of the then unexplored Atlantic) shall be kept for this purpose of which I am speaking. The hardy Norsemen may navigate its seas and touch upon its shores, but I shall frustrate every attempt to colonize. It 'shall wait for me' until a great Christian people shall need it to flee to from spiritual bondage and oppression, and start the embryo of my Christian Israel, and then, Israel, 'the ships of Tarshish' shall be 'first to bring thy sons from far.'"

It was a fact constantly kept in mind by all of Gods'

Prophets, even at that early day, that "westward the course of empire takes its ways." Hence the Prophet knew that the glorious nation, which he was describing, was in the west, and hence, according to his knowledge of geography, must be in the region known as the "isles." "The ships of Tarshish"—Tarshish, as you all know, was the most ancient name of Spain. "Ships of Tarshish *first*." As prophecy notes only the greatest events of time, the term "first" must apply to some very important and famous circumstance. America answers to the "waiting isles," and "the ships of Tarshish first to bring thy sons," to the discovery of America by the ships of Spain. It has always seemed very strange to us that America was not colonized before it was; that this great and rich continent, capable of sustaining such a vast population, should lie here unoccupied, and that, too, when the population of Europe was so dense and needed this continent to spread out in. But God plainly tells us in this Prophecy that He preserved it until His Christian Israel was strong enough and the time had arrived for them to take possession and build up a great Christian republic, which should develop into the millennial kingdom. "*Surely* the isles shall wait for me"; the words "surely" and "me" plainly show that He *intentionally* reserved it for His own purposes. Again, Ezek. xlvii. 13: "Ye shall inherit the land according to the twelve tribes of Israel; Joseph shall have two portions." Joseph had two portions of old Israel, and thus there were thirteen tribes; and here we are informed that the same number was to exist at the rise of Christian Israel. In the next chapter, the 48th, it is said these divisions shall lie side by side on a great sea, with their limits extending from sea to sea, "from the east side unto the west side" of the continent. Now, is it not an astonishing fulfillment of prophecy, when we see the United States taking its rise in twelve colonies, and William Penn, like Joseph, having two ceded to him, making thirteen in all, and they lying side by side on a great sea? But it is truly *overpowering* evidence of fulfillment, when we see that the language of the old charters was that they should "extend *westward* from sea to sea."

Again, Isaiah ii. 2-3: "And it shall come to pass, in the last days, that the mountain of the Lord's house shall be established in the top of the mountains and shall be exhalted above the hills, and all nations shall flow unto it, and many people shall go and say, 'come ye and let us go up to the mountain of the Lord, to the house of the God of Jacob.'" The term "mountain" in the prophecies invariably means government of some kind, either civil or ecclesiastical. The expression "last days" signifies the Christian era; in this place it means the time from the rise of Christian Israel to the coming of Christ. The expression, "let us *go up* to the mountain (or nationality) of the Lord," intimates that its locality shall be elevated, and Lieutenant Maury shows that the whole earth, to reach us, is literally obliged to *come up* to us. We are on the physical head of the world. The gulf stream runs at the rate of four miles an hour across the whole breadth of the Atlantic. The expression, "all nations shall flow unto it," does not mean *simply* that emigrants shall come from all nations to it, as they do indeed to us, but that all nations, as nations, shall ultimately flow into it. It will eventually absorb all the kingdoms of the world. As St. John says, in speaking of a later period of Israel restored, when the seventh trumpet sounded, "there were great voices in heaven saying, 'the kingdoms of this world are become the kingdoms of our Lord and of His Christ, and He shall reign forever and ever.'"

Ezek. xxxviii. 8: "After many days thou shalt be visited; in the later years thou shalt come into the land that is brought back from the sword and is gathered out of many people against the mountains of Israel, which have been always waste; but it is brought forth out of the nations, and they shall dwell safely all of them." The expression, "after many days," is explained in the next line by the expression, "in the latter years." He tells us in this verse that Christian Israel shall be restored in a land which has "been *always* waste." What land can answer to this but America, and the world has all been explored and there is no rich section lying waste of sufficient extent in which to found a great empire, as Israel restored must of necessity be. He says again, "it is brought forth out of the nations." This is not the same as the similar expression in this Prophecy, "gathered out of many people," and in the 12th verse of this chapter, "gathered out of many nations," an expression so frequently used by the Prophets in speaking of the nationality of Christian Israel, but this expression, "brought forth *out* of the nations," means that it had its rise outside of the nations, (not founded on other empires, etc.,) a characteristic of Christian Israel which runs through all the predictions of it. You will please note this fact in the further progress of this subject. That this is the intended meaning is further seen in the expression that follows. "And they shall dwell safely all of them," means that their position in the earth shall be such that they shall not be easy of access to other nations, that their natural fastnesses shall be like the great Atlantic and Pacific.

In the 8th verse, as we have seen, God was addressing Israel; in the 11th and 12th, He addresses "Gog." Gog and Magog are put for the enemies of Israel in the "latter days." "Gog" is derived from "Magog," and literally means a "prince" or "ruler." He is called a prince or head of many countries. They are both symbolic terms, and are meant to represent Israel's enemies. Hence God addresses him "thou" (Gog). I would premise, before quoting this, that God is speaking of a later period than the rise of Israel. He is speaking here of the great battle of Armageddon, which ushers in the millennium. "Thou (Gog) shalt say, I will go up to the land of unwalled villages; I will go to them that are at rest, that dwell safely, all of them dwelling without walls, and having neither bars nor gates; to turn thy hand upon the desolate places that are now inhabited, upon the people that are gathered out of the nations." Here we have the same expression, "I will *go up* to the land." This expression is always used when speaking of approach to Christian Israel. "The land of unwalled villages, dwelling without walls, and having neither bars nor gates, finds its complete fulfillment with us. The phrase, "at rest, that dwell safely, etc.," refers again to their being a distance from other nations. We are "the desolate places that are now inhabited;" we are "the people that are gathered out of the nations."

Isaiah xlix. 23: "Kings shall be thy nursing fathers and queens thy nursing mothers." The word "nursing" in the margin is translated "nourishers." These terms imply attentions to the infancy of the restoration. If it had not been for the attentions of royalty in our early history, we could not have survived. From the time Isabella sold her jewels, through all our weak and dependent history, they were our support. Mr. Baldwin says: "The memorial of nursing kings and queens and princes will remain upon our rivers and waters, our counties and towns, our cities and States, while time shall last. Louisiana, Georgia, the Carolinas, Virginia, Maryland, Delaware, New York, New Jersey and New Hampshire will ever suggest the early interest of royalty in our colonial history."

Isaiah i. 26: "I will restore thy judges as at the first, and thy counselors as at the *beginning*." This shows emphatically what kind of a government Christian Israel shall be. It shall be like the Hebrew republic in the beginning, not after they had wickedly changed it into a monarchy. Judges and counselors were an essential part of Hebrew democracy, or of the *first* government, the one *God* established for them, and it shows emphatically that their restoration implies republicanism.

Jere. xxx. 21: "Their nobles shall be of themselves, and their governor from the midst of them." What country but ours will answer to this? No comment of ours will enlighten this. Isaiah xlvii. 17: "Thy destroyers, and they that make thee waste, shall go forth of thee." The principles of monarchy in any form, spiritual or civil, have always wasted the true Christian Church. The abandoning of Christian Israel by all monarchies leaves the only alternative of freedom. But the great destroyer of the true Christian Church has been the papal power, which is called in Revelations "the beast;" called by St. Paul "that man of sin, the son of perdition, who," he says, "opposeth and exalteth himself above all that is called God or that is worshiped, so that he, as God, sitteth in the temple of God, showing himself that he is God." And since he has arrogated to himself infallibility, how completely he fulfills these predictions of him. Now, the prophecy we are considering, I believe to be a promise that Christian Israel *shall be* freed from this element so hostile to civil and religious liberty. Now there are two ways in which this may be brought about. One is by war and bloodshed, and the other is by their becoming Americanized by being brought in contact with our systems of enlightenment, our public schools, our teaching of pure Gospel doctrines, and our free institutions. Some fear the former; I do not. I believe it will be brought about in the last mentioned way. God does not save people by churches and societies and corporate bodies, but individually. Human salvation is an individual concernment; hence there are many good people in the Romish Church, and thousands are being saved out of it constantly; and no class of people, however deep they may be sunk in ignorance and superstition, can be brought in contact with our systems of enlightenment and free institutions, without coming up out of the wilderness. And this is the reason why some, who want to keep the masses in subjection to them, and consequently try to keep them in ignorance, are so hostile to our public school system and free institutions in general.

We are aware that great efforts are put forth, and Cardinals are sent over, but we will enlighten their masses, Americanize and Christianize them, and make good subjects of Christian Israel of them. Some of their leaders and some few bigoted members, who refuse to advance with progressive America (or Israel), will finally leave our Israel of their own accord, as a soil not congenial to the growth of their principles. Fear not, my American citizens; fear not the bloody inquisition, nor the power of the beast and the dragon, in any form, for the promise has gone forth from Jehovah, "thy destroyers shall go forth of thee."

Again, Isaiah xxxiii. 20: "Thine eyes shall see Jerusalem a quiet habitation, a tabernacle that shall not be taken down; but there the glorious Lord shall be unto us a place of broad rivers and streams, wherein shall go no galley with oars, neither shall gallant ships pass thereby." The term Jerusalem is used as often as the term Israel to designate God's nationality. It is a circumstance to be noted, that whenever the Prophets speak of the restoration of Israel, they always express in some form its peace and permanency. Here it is expressed in the sentence, "Thine eyes shall see Jerusalem a quiet habitation, a tabernacle that shall not be taken down." "A place of broad rivers and streams," implies a land of great prosperity and peace. Mr. Baldwin says: "It is common in Scripture to embody a promise or threat in terms figurative, which, when taken literally, designate the very agencies by which the threat or promise is realized. Sword and fire may symbolize war, or rain may represent plenty, yet each is an essential agent in the realization. So, broad rivers and streams may symbolize vast inland prosperity, and yet are essential means in effecting it, and may, therefore, be taken in a literal as well as figurative sense." "Galley" and "gallant ship" represent the greater and smaller classes of war vessels. Their presence would indicate the vassalage of Jerusalem to foreigners; their absence, therefore, declares Israel's independence. Vast inland prosperity, afforded by broad rivers and streams, a glorious independence of all nations, are great features of Christian Israel and of the American people.

. Daniel says: "Unto 2300 days, then shall the sanctuary be cleansed. It shall be for a time, times and a half, and when he shall have accomplished, to scatter the power of the holy people, all these things shall be finished. From the time the daily sacrifice shall be taken away, there shall be 1290 days." These texts give each the length of Israel's desolation. Their starting point is at the cessation of the daily sacrifice on the 189th day of the year 68 A. D. Dr. Baldwin shows conclusively that their ending is on July 4th, 1776. On that day a nation was born.

CHAPTER II.

We propose in this chapter to examine Nebuchadnezzar's celebrated vision of the great monarchy image. This vision was given 605 years B. C., or in the year of the world 3401. This prophecy contains a history of the world from that period to the millennium. It is recorded in Dan. II. and reads as follows: "Thou, O king, sawest, and behold a great image. This great image, whose brightness was excellent, stood before thee; and the form thereof was terrible." "This image's head was of fine gold, his breast and his arms of silver, his belly and his thighs of brass." "His legs of iron, his feet part of iron and part of clay." "Thou sawest till that a stone was cut without hands, which smote the image upon his feet that were of iron and clay, and brake them in pieces." "Then was the iron, the clay, the brass, the silver, and the gold, broken to pieces together, and became like the chaff of the summer threshing-floors; and the wind carried them away, that no place was found for them: and the stone that smote the image became a great mountain, and filled the whole earth." This image is the embodiment of all the great monarchial governments that were ever to exist, for so the Prophet affirms. Now you will observe that this image expresses chronology from the head downward, and as the Prophet gives the first one, there is no trouble in recognizing each successive kingdom as they arise, for they arise in chronological order, and occupy the same territory. "This image's head was of fine gold," and the Prophet says: "*Thou art this head of gold.*" Here the first kingdom is *expressly* stated by the Prophet to be the Babylonian empire. He says this empire embraced the whole earth, "wheresoever the children of men dwell, the beasts of the field," etc., God "hath made thee ruler over them all," implies universal dominion. Its capital was in Asia. It subdued a portion of Africa. Carried its conquests into Europe as far as Spain. It was not literally universal, but according to Daniel's interpretation, it was sufficiently so to answer the purposes of prophecy. Again, "This image's head was of fine gold, his breast and his arms of silver." Now Daniel says, "Thou art this head of gold, and after thee shall arise another kingdom inferior to thee." The first kingdom being given, and the next following in chronological order, and was to supply the place of the other, and occupy the same territory, it is easy to discover the name of the second as soon as it made its appearance. Media and Persia were originally provinces of the Assyrian empire, and in the day of Cyrus they were united in one monarchy, and overturned the Babylonian empire, and of course this was the second empire intended by Daniel, since it removed the first and raised itself upon its ruins. Hence the "Medo-Persian" empire was the second, or silver empire.

The Prophet says, the "Medo-Persian" empire was to be inferior to the first, which history corroborates. It was inferior, both in extent of empire and morally. We will not spend much time identifying the four kingdoms of monarchy, they are so very easy to identify, and all modern writers on the Prophecies, as far as we are acquainted, agree as to these four empires. The third kingdom is that represented by the *brass:* The interpretation says, "Thou art this head of gold, and after thee shall arise another kingdom inferior to thee, and another third kingdom of *brass*, which shall bear rule over all the earth." Alexander the Great subverted the Persian empire and founded the Macedonian on its ruins. So the third kingdom that appeared in chronological order from the Babylonian was the Macedonian. It will be observed that no two of these kingdoms *could* exist at one and the same time, for each one was to be universal, hence *had* to occupy the same territory. So each successor was, therefore, compelled to overthrow its predecessor to make room for itself. The character of this empire was symbolized by the brass. Bishop Newton says, "the Macedonian empire was fitly represented by brass, for the Greeks were famous for their brazen armor, their usual epithet being, 'The Brazen-coated Greeks.'" But we think more important qualities were intended by the metal. Dr. Baldwin says, "the gold of the head indicated the refined character, splendor and value of the Babylonian empire; and the silver, the inferior value and splendor of the Persian power; the brass, being baser yet stronger than gold or silver, may indicate a baser moral character of government, but of greater energies and capabilities in war." Again, the third kingdom was to bear rule over all the earth. The term "all the earth" has various significations in the scriptures. It generally means the civilized world, and this empire comprised "all the earth" as extensively as the Babylonian, and Daniel says, that was sufficiently universal to answer the prophecy. It is said that Alexander's empire comprehended Europe, Asia and Africa as largely as any empire ever did, except the Roman, and that was subsequent. It is related of Alexander that after he had subverted the Medo-Persian empire, he stood upon the shore of the Indian ocean and wept that there were no more to conquer. It was doubtless at this time in his history that he gave command that he should be called "king of the world." Alexander conquered in obedience to his unbounded ambition, not knowing that he was putting in a link in prophecy when he did it. Again, the later existence of the third kingdom was to be marked by a division into two branches; this is indicated by the brass extending from the body into the limbs. Now, it is a well known fact in history, that after Alexander's death the Macedonian empire was divided among his four officers, Cassander, Lysymachus, Ptolemy, Seleucus. But these were soon reduced to two, Legidæ and Seleucidæ reigning in Syria and Egypt.

Bishop Newton says: "Their kingdom was no more a different kingdom than the parts differ from the whole. It was the same government still continued. They who governed were still Macedonians. The metal was the same, and the nation was the same. Nor is the same nation ever represented by different metals, but the different metals always signify different nations. All ancient authors speak of the kingdom of Alexander and his successors as one and the same kingdom. The thing is implied in the very name by which they are called, *the successors of Alexander*. But perhaps we have spent time enough on this kingdom to identify it as the Macedonian.

We come now to the fourth—the iron kingdom, or Roman empire. Interpretation: "And the fourth kingdom shall be strong as iron; forasmuch as iron breaketh, all these shall it break in pieces and bruise, and whereas thou sawest the feet and toes, part of potters' clay and part of iron, the kingdom shall be divided. But there shall be in it of the strength of the iron, forasmuch as thou sawest the iron mixed with miry clay. And as the toes of the feet were part of iron and part of clay, so the kingdom shall be partly strong and partly broken. And whereas thou sawest iron mixed with clay, THEY shall mingle themselves with the seed of men. But they shall not cleave one to another, even as iron is no mixed with clay. Thou sawest till that a stone was cut ou without hands, which smote the image upon his *feet, that* were of iron and clay, and brake them in pieces." This kingdom is represented by the symbol as existing in three distinct forms. The first form is that of a unit, represented by the iron alone. "His legs were of iron." It was, you observe, purely an iron kingdom for a period of time. As each metal was a little stronger than the preceding one, as you come down the image in chronological order, showing the power of each kingdom to subvert its predecessor, so it is expressly stated that "the fourth kingdom shall be strong as iron, forasmuch as iron breaketh, all these [kingdoms or metals] shall it break in pieces and bruise." One writer says: "Rome has the best claim to this iron character of any nation that ever existed; whether consolidated or in fragments, it has wielded greater power and commanded a larger measure of influence, been more resistless in war and endured more lastingly, than any other empire whatever. It was a vast kingdom of warror, and that, too, for ages. And Mars was its tutelary deity. Its code of jurisprudence also have yielded a commanding influence in the earth for near two thousand years. As iron is the strongest of metals, so Rome has been the strongest of all nations." The fourth kingdom was to crush out all other nations. The Roman empire comprehended all of the civilized world and much of the barbarous. The three eastern continents were within it, or tributary to it.

In our Saviour's time the term Rome and the whole earth were used as synonymous terms. St. Luke says, when our Saviour was born a decree had gone forth from Cæsar Augustus that "all the world should be taxed." Rome existed as an iron unit down to the days of Theodosius, or for a thousand years. Now, we come to the second form in which this kingdom existed. Now, you will observe, that the composition or material that symbolized each kingdom, symbolized its political character. So with this last kingdom, after it existed purely an iron kingdom for a while, another element, another material comes in with the iron. Of all the expositors, but one has treated with any critical attention the coming in of the clay. By this it is evident that the union of Church and State is intended. That the clay symbolizes a class of people, the same as the metals, not only stands to reason, but is put beyond a *doubt* by the Prophet's *own* interpretation. He says, in referring to the clay, "THEY"—mark you, he uses the pronoun of multitude, "THEY," referring to people. "They shall mingle with the seed of men." By the expression, "seed of men," is implied men of the world, or political world. A similar expression is found in the VI chap. 2d verse of Genesis, where it means the same. Again, as the iron unquestionably represented the political character of the empire before the clay came in with the iron and mixes with it in about equal proportions, and as this class of men represented by the clay, and designated by the pronoun "*they*," are said by the Prophets to "mingle themselves with that class represented by the iron, they *must of necessity* conjointly represent the political character of the empire after this union. And the Prophet also says that these two classes of men though united in the government, "shall not cleave one to another even as iron is not mixed [chemically] with clay." And as to the peace and harmony of this incestuous union of Church and State, I will refer you to all past history. . Dr. Baldwin has very well said: "As the clay is a base material, so the Christian Church, by this union with the State, has been grossly corrupted, and they who mingled themselves with the seed of men have become baser than the iron of the world. As the clay and iron were not to cleave closely to each other, so has been this debased alloy of Church and State. The exact relationship of the Church to the State has never been generally agreed upon, and there has been through past ages a constant struggle between them for political supremacy, the iron generally prevailing over the clay. Popes have arrogated supremacy, and absolved subjects from allegiance to kings and princes; but kings and princes have generally carried the day. So, that while they have remained and do remain combined, they have never been united, even "as iron is not [chemically] united or mixed with clay." They have had conflicting interests, and, from the nature of the case, they always will have.

Nothing can exceed the accuracy of the brief description the Prophet gives of Church and State union in the Roman empire since it institution. Nothing, in fact, could be more perfect. The Church, with her magical cross, has awed kings and princes, rulers and people, into submission. The Pope has brought kings to his feet, and powerful emperors have spent frosty nights in penance upon his door-step. While kings and emperors in return, rising from their magic spell, as from the deep of slumber, have, while gratifying their own ambition, thought it best to curb the ambition of the Pope, and with the sword have—in the language of the great Napoleon—"brought his highness to terms." While God intends that a pure and enlightened religion, or Christianity, shall be the mother of a perfect civil government in the earth, He evidently does not intend the union of Church and State. *That* has ever been fruitful of the greatest evil. While carnal Israel, or the Jewish Church, reaped some advantages by her bondage in Egypt and connection with Pharoah's throne, drawing her supplies from the government, was preserved from famine, multiplied in numbers, etc. So spiritual Israel, or the Christian Church gained some advantage at first, in going into spiritual bondage, by being connected with the throne of the Roman empire. But since that day, blood and crime has marked her way in the earth. Aside from the terrible wars she has engendered, the lands she has desolated, the homes she has saddened, it is estimated that 50,000,000 souls have lost their lives by her union with the State.

I have before stated, and I hope to show beyond a doubt, before I get through with this present vision of Daniel. That when a great and mighty nation suddenly arose on the 4th day of July, 1776, civil and religious liberty first dawned upon the world, by the complete and eternal divorcement of Church and State.

Up to that time we read of the horrid inquisitions, auto-defe, bloody massacres. But since that day that hellish trio, Pope, Pagan and Despot, with their concommitants, the rack, the wheel, the stake and the guillotine, have all felt that at our dawn, humanity arose, and with that humanity, a *civil arm* that will not brook such horrid means to force the impenetrable entrenchments of the human soul; to bind down the unconquerable human conscience; to put out the unquenchable flame that burns in the human heart for civil and religious liberty.

We have shown these kingdoms to be the Babylonian, Medo-ersian, Macedonian and Roman. We have seen that the profane historian agrees with revelation in pointing out these kingdoms. Prophecy is history pre-written, hence, the true Prophet and the correct historian must agree. Bishop Newton says: "All ancient writers, both Jewish and Christian, agree with Jerome in explaining the fourth kingdom to be the Roman." Mr. Mede says: "The Roman empire, to be the fourth kingdom of Daniel, was believed by the Church of Israel, both before and in our Saviour's time; received by the disciples of the Apostles and the whole Christian Church, for the first three hundred years, without any *known* contradictions. And I confess, having so good ground in Scripture, it is with me " *Tantvm non est articulus fidei,"* little less than an article of faith. Now, the third form, or period, of this kingdom was the broken one represented by the ten toes. Mark, these two things are affirmed of this kingdom: It was to be divided and then broken. It was to be divided into Church and State (clay and iron) after continuing for a period; it was to be broken up into smaller kingdoms, and its political character of clay and iron was to continue in its broken state, the clay continues with the iron down into the toes. The Roman empire was broken to pieces by the inroads of the Germans, Goths, Vandals and Huns, and ten kingdoms in less than two hundred years made their appearance. These ten were simply a representative number. There were to be many more than these during its broken period. Rome is still in its broken state, characterized still by the union of Church and State (clay and iron.) Now, there is this difference between the Prophet and the Historian —the Prophet looks upon the Roman empire as still existing in its broken state; the Historian, as having passed away, and its place supplied by smaller ones. Now, the Prophet intimates that it is to be reunited or consolidated again. *This* must be his meaning, for he says, the stone, or the fifth kingdom, smote the image on the feet, which *must* have been after it had existed for a period in that state represented by the toes.

If I understand Dr. Baldwin, he thinks it is to be restored as it was before. I do not think so. I think by *this* is meant the confederation of all these monarchies, preparatory to the great blow to be struck against republicanism, or, as it is called in prophecy, the great battle of "*Armageddon,*" sybolized here by the stone kingdom, of which we purpose to speak in the next chapter.

Let us mark this one particular, as we pass from the time these kingdoms began to rise, the march of empire has been steadily *westward.* We will see when we come to treat of the next, the fifth or stone kingdom, that "the star of empire" has not changed her course, but that

> "Westward the course of empire takes its way,
> The first four acts already passed.
> The fifth shall close the drama with the day,
> Time's noblest empire is its last."

CHAPTER III.

We will all agree, doubtless, in the beginning of this investigation, upon this one fact: That this fifth kingdom which the vision presents, and which Daniel interprets, is no other, and *can* be no other, than the restoration of Israel to nationality. For it is here doing precisely the work that is always predicted of Israel restored; that is, breaking in pieces and subduing monarchy, or, in the variable language of the Prophets, subduing all the kingdoms of the world.

Again, it occupies the same territory that Israel was to occupy, and that is the whole entire world, and also its endless duration, which is here expressed in that same language so often used by the Prophets "for ever and ever." You must have observed all along, how careful the Prophets are in speaking of Christian Israel's nationality, to not leave the subject without speaking of its universality and perpetuity. You can invariably detect that the Prophets are speaking of this nationality by these two features. Something that cannot be said— of course—of any other nation that may ever arise; for it comprises the whole world and shall endure "forever." This kingdom, as you are aware, we claim to be the United States of America.

You may say we are treading a new path for truth. Not wholly so. The late president of the "Soule Female College," a man of no mean talent, held the same views that we do. We are aware of the difficulties and disadvantages under which we labor in expounding prophecy. But, the difficulties are not in the prophecies, especially those that have been unsealed to man by a partial fulfillment. But they lie in the preconceived opinions of men upon the subject, and the firm and settled error of those opinions, and the determined hostility to any argument that would overthrow or unsettle them. Dr. Whedon, the commentator says, "every man is in an exegetical fix," the difficulty is, to get him out of that fix, and get new and correct opinions into him.

A celebrated educator has said, "it is harder to unlearn what we have learned wrong than to learn correctly." One author says, "some persons have never fully formed an opinion on the subject; while others have satisfied themselves that some one has made a great mistake in explaining prophecy somehow, and are consequently distrustful of the ability of any man to throw any new light upon the subject. Others and of the smaller class, are ever ready fairly to examine all honorable argument and to decide justly. And as for ourselves, we can truly say, we had rather, by far, try to make a wide-awake, progressive infidel see these sublime truths, than *some* who have been rocked in the cradle of Christianity, for they will tell you that the old elder who baptized their great grand-father, and preached to four generations down from him, never interpreted Scripture that way. And you might as well try to shake Mt. Ætna down into a plain, as to enrich their minds with any new discoveries in Scripture.

But to return; please pardon this digression. We will take up the points which are given to identify this kingdom.

1st. The time of its rise. This is expressed and implied in the positive words of the vision and in the interpretation, also, in the time when the destruction of the image was to take place. The Prophet says: "Thou sawest *till* that a stone was cut out without hands." Now, mark closely the following fact: "It is certain that the image was a chronological one and represented successive kingdoms, from the Babylonian down to the broken state of the Roman empire represented by toes of iron and clay. *It is certain* that he saw the history of the world down to the subversion of the Roman empire. *It is certain* that he saw a period of time extending from his day down to the fifth century. *It is certain* that after he had seen the whole era of the image down to the broken stages of Rome, that he continued to look prospectively into the future. *It is certain* that he did not see the empire of the stone until he had seen the whole history of the world from his own days to those of the broken empire. *Nor did he see it then*, for *it is certain* that he saw it by looking beyond the period of the broken state of Rome, and that he did not see it by any retrospective view. That little episode thrown in there, "*thou sawest till,*" has an expressiveness of futurity in it absolutely, as well as relatively. The word *till*, says Mr. Webster, signifies "to the time of, or, to the time, as, I will wait *till* next week, or, occupy *till* I come." Now, the Prophet expressly told the King, that *after* he had seen the whole prophetic and chronological image, down to the toes or broken state, that he then continued to look *forward*, and that in looking his attention was arrested by the sight of a stone cut out of the mountains without hands. "This view is further confirmed, as well as illustrated, by a parallel and fac-simile passage found in Daniel's vision of the very same events. After Daniel saw the broken state of the fourth kingdom, he says, he continued to look into the future, and then he uses the same style of language," "I beheld till the thrones were cast down." This expression and the one before us, "thou sawest *till*" the stone kingdom destroyed monarchy, synchronize and relate to the same events. The Prophet's own interpretation of the vision drives us to the same conclusio irresistibly. He says: "In the days of these kings shall the God of heaven set up a kingdom," etc. We have authorit that the Hebrew original " beyomahon" signified literally, "i their days." These plural terms show us plainly that it was after the broken state of Rome, after the ten representativ kingdoms had arisen. Some refer these words to the four preceding kingdoms. But this must, of necessity, be incorrect. The fifth kingdom could smite the Babylonish king, the Persian, the Macedonian and the Roman, but it could not smite *kings* in this case, for they reigned centuries apart; but the Prophet is speaking of a number of kingdoms existing simultaneously. He gives us the history of the image chronologically down to the toe or broken period, when there are several kings reigning at the same time, and then he says: "In the days of these kings," etc. Again, in speaking of the power of the fifth kingdom, he says: "It shall brake in pieces and consume all *these kingdoms.*" Now, I ask you what is plainer than this fact, that if this fifth kingdom had arisen in the days of Rome, before it was broken into a plurality of kingdoms, that it must have been set up in the days of *one* king, or kingdom, and *not* "in *their* days of *these* kings," as the text says it should be. Again, it is a principle of logic that "relative words should be referred to the nearest, rather than to a remote, antecedent," hence we cannot, therefore, without a palpable violation of a plain, logical rule, make the terms in "*their* days and of those kings," refer to the great period of the whole four kingdoms.

2d. We come now to *the origin of the stone kingdom.* No one but Dr. Baldwin ever interpreted one vastly important symbol, which we now bring forward. It is perfectly astonishing that all writers on the Prophecies, prior to Mr. Baldwin, should have passed by unnoticed this most important of all the symbols. And that is the *mountain origin* of the stone kingdom. The vision says: "Thou sawest till a stone was cut out without hands." Here it is very plain that the stone was inherent in *something*, otherwise it would not have been " cut out." The Prophet's interpretation says it was "cut *out of* the mountain." As the stone symbolically represented a kingdom, and a very powerful one to destroy such powerful empires, it is plain that the stone kingdom was derived from some pre-existing power, from which such a powerful kingdom could be cut or formed. Now, it was cut from *the mountain*, and the term mountain has a definite meaning in the Prophecies, and always signifies an organized body of people of some kind, either political or ecclesiastical.

"Now, the fifth kingdom being cut out of a prophetic kingdom, we must inquire what kind of government it was to be. It was evident, from the nature of the case, that it was a kingdom totally different from any in the image represented by the gold, silver, clay, iron or brass. It is further clear that as the stone would partake of the nature of its original composition, that the mountain would be opposed in character to the kingdoms in the image, because the stone kingdom hated and destroyed the other kingdoms. Now, the only great organization in the world that hates corrupt religion and corrupt civil government is pure and free Christianity, and therefore the mountain must represent the true Church or kingdom of Christ." Hence, the fifth or stone kingdom is that nation which has arisen out of Christianity, freed from Church and State union, or out of the "mountain of the Lord's house." Of those who hold that the stone kingdom is Christianity, I would not only ask such persons what the mountain is that the stone kingdom is cut out of, but I would inform such that Christianity is forbidden to do the work of the stone kingdom. To break in pieces and consume powerful kingdoms requires a powerful martial force; and the founder of Christianity said: "Put up thy sword; he that taketh the sword, let him perish by the sword," etc. And if you say Christianity did this by working internally, we shall show you before we get through with this subject that that stone came from a distance and smote it on the outside. Mark one more thing: The term "*cut out* of the mountain" does not imply a part *cut off* from the mountain, as a stone cut off from a cliff or ledge of rocks composing a mountain, but the change of the mountain substance into a double nature, just as we say a statue is cut out of a block of marble, or a vase is cut out of alabaster. Again, the stone kingdom is identified by its *political character*. We have already intimated, and it is plainly seen from the prophecy, that this fifth empire was to possess a mighty political strength of character. If you were to listen to a man reading history, and he should read of one powerful kingdom after another, each wielding a powerful martial force, overthrowing other kingdoms, at a great expense of life and treasure; and all at once he should mention one doing the same work, and he should stop and say to you: "This is spiritual, *not* a political, organization," you would want to know what authority he had for that interpretation.

We wish to quote to you on this point Mr. Tillinghast, in full. He says the kingdom of the stone is a kingdom in respect of nature, the same with the kingdoms represented by the great image, *i. e.*, it is outward as they are outward, which appears:

1st. From the general scope and drift of the prophecy, which runs upon outward kingdoms. All the first four kingdoms, or monarchies, are outward, as none can deny; why, then, the Holy Ghost, in speaking of the fifth and last, should so vary the scope as to glide from the outward kingdom to the inward, ought (besides the bare say-so) to have some solid and substantial reason brought for it by those, *whosoever* they are, that either do or shall assert it.

2d. Because it is not proper to say, that a bare spiritual kingdom, considered only as spiritual, should break in pieces, beat to very chaff, *grind to powder* the great image, i. e., destroy the very being of worldly kingdoms, which work is yet, notwithstanding, done by the stone. Indeed Christ's spiritual kingdom may, by that light and life which it gives forth, much refine and reform outward kingdoms, but when once the work comes to breaking to pieces, i. e., subverting kingdoms, razing their very foundations and destroying their very being, as they are the kings of this world here, unless we conceive God to do it by a miracle, must we also conceive some other hand, besides a spiritual, to be put to the work.

3d. Because the stone, to the end there might not be a vacancy in the world, comes straightway in the place and room of the great image, so soon as the same is totally broken. For as the great image, while standing, bears rule over all the earth, so the same being broken, the stone becomes a mountain, and fills the whole earth, therefore must the kingdom of the stone be such a kingdom, as was that of the great image. Viz., *Outward:* or otherwise, the coming of that, in the place of the other now taken away, could not supply the want of the other." We quote from Baldwin:

1st. "The nature of the work to be accomplished by the stone was of a purely political, or rather material character. It was to break up the four great monarchies, and utterly anhihilate them. No monarchy was ever broken down except by martial or political violence; and no kingdom was ever overthrown by another without great bloodshed. The vision says, the fifth kingdom shall break the four kingdoms to pieces, and they should become as chaff; the interpretation says, 'it shall break in pieces and consume all these kingdoms.' Here the stone is stated to perform the work of annihilation of the political fabrics before it, in two ways: first by breaking them to pieces; and, secondly, by consuming them.

The term, "breaking to pieces," must be understood in the same sense in which the Prophet uses it in other parts of the prophecy. Now, he said of the fourth kingdom of iron, that it should "break in pieces" all the kingdoms before it. Then, as the Roman, or fourth kingdom, broke in pieces all the nations before it, by the most bloody and devastating wars, it follows, that as the fourth kingdom should be "broken to pieces" by the stone, that the breaking would, in its case, be by dreadful war, as in the other cases. There is no room to evade this conclusion without violating a plain rule of interpretation; that is, by assigning a different sense to an author's words than he himself has given. The terms, "became chaff," and "consuming," are obviously somewhat different in signification from that of "breaking to pieces." They imply that the empire was first divided into large masses, and that these were then subjugated and utterly wasted away by conquest.

St. John, in describing the destruction of the Roman power in the last battles, by the fifth kingdom, says the beast and false phophet were first taken, and then the remnant were slain. The beast corresponds to the fourth kingdom; and he being taken, coincides with the breaking up of the image into fragments; and the slaying of the remnant coincides with the consuming process upon the fragments of the broken image.

2d. The breaking of the image was by a sudden stroke of the stone. Dr. Adam Clark says, the falling of the stone upon the feet of the image was like the stroke of a stone discharged violently from a Roman catapult. There was but one stroke of the stone on the feet. It was plainly a swift stroke, and, therefore, a sudden one; there was no protracted effort on its part to break up monarchy; there was no repetition of the blow by the stone, for the image fell the very instant its feet felt the force of the single disrupting blow. The text says, it "smote the image upon his feet, which were of iron and clay, and broke them to pieces;" and it adds, "then was the iron, the clay, the brass, the silver, and the gold broken to pieces together." One sudden stroke of the stone broke the feet to pieces, and then, at that very time, for such is the meaning of the term then, the whole material fell to pieces. The sudden dashing of the Roman empire to pieces by a single stroke, absolutely implies great and unprecedented political or martial power. And, again, the existence of the empire in fragments, implies that this state was produced by political power; and its comminution into chaff is still further expressive of it.

3d. The time when this smiting was to transpire, is further proof that the fifth kingdom was to be a political power. The feet were to be broken by the stone, and then every vestige of Rome was to disappear. The *toes* were not to be smitten, but the *feet*, the Prophet says. Now, as the image was chronological, the Roman empire represented by the toes, was not simultaneous with that state of it represented by the feet, nor could the image be smitten in that state represented by the feet prior to that represented by the toes; for if it had been, the toe, or broken state, would never have appeared at all, because the image was all to dissolve at only one stroke of the stone. The only way to reconcile the matter, is, by allowing a reunion of the broken empire represented by the feet of iron and clay. St. John clearly states, that the ten kingdoms should agree together to give their power to the beast, and that, in this confederacy, they should be broken by the fifth empire; he, therefore, fully confirms our positions here. No man of any brains can imagine that the European states, when confederated, can ever be broken to pieces by an extraneous power, unless that extraneous power be a civil government with martial power.

4th. The Roman empire, or fourth kingdom, was to be demolished by a power without its borders. The stone was not in any wise attached to the image; it was not generated in it, and did not operate upon the image internally; it smote the image outside, and moved toward it from a distance. It was, therefore, a kingdom that did not grow up in the bounds of the Roman empire at all; it did not foment discord in its territories or secretly and silently work its ruin by *moral suasion*. On the contrary, as it grew in strength, Rome grew in strength; for as it originated in the broken state of Rome, and did not smite it till Rome was reunited, it is evident that both grew stronger simultaneously. It was an external, foreign power to Rome or Europe, and its country was not in the limits of the old Roman empire.

5th. The kingdom of the mountain, into which the stone was to grow, every one admits, will be a government in which everything will be Christianized. From the very nature of the case, the civil and spiritual departments of good government will never be blended. Christ will ultimately be priest of the one and king of the other; but this does not imply that they will ever be blended, but just the contrary. The millennial government, or mountain will, therefore, possess a civil department. Now, as the kingdom of the stone is simply to expand into the millennial government, it follows that it must be possessed of a civil department of government. Those persons who fancy a universal church on earth, with no civil code, have very crude notions of the matter, to say the least of it. Mr. Baldwin says: "The gospel will never admit of any such universal salmagundi."

CHAPTER IV.

In the last chapter we considered some of the features of the fifth or stone kingdom, its rise, origin, and its character to some extent. Now, there is nothing more evident than the fact that this stone kingdom possessed a mighty political or martial power, for without it it could not have done the work predicted of it. By the smiting of the stone in the vision is symbolized the great battle of Armageddon, spoken of in Revelation 16th chap., 14th, 15th and 16th verses, as the *great and decisive* struggle of republicanism with monarchy. Of the place and time and particulars of this terrible war we will try to speak more definitely in another treatise. But after the stone kingdom had accomplished the mammoth work of destroying all the political powers of the East, it grew into a *great* mountain (a great nationality), and filled the whole earth. It had to do this of necessity, to supply the place of the others, it had to extend its own form of government over them. The prophet tells us this stone kingdom was God's government, one He established, and we have already seen that the only government that God *claims* to have established on earth was a republic, and He has promised that, that nation restored shall be of the same style of government. It is apparent to human reason, that God's church—that is, Christianity—must eventually give to the world, and the whole world, a civil code; and the only form of government that *free* Christianity heartily endorses is the democratic. Now, it is certain, that not only the work, but the nature and power of the stone kingdom, proves it to be Israel res'ored, but its universality and perpetuity puts it beyond a doubt. *But one* kingdom can be universal and of endless duration. The stone after it became a great nation, and filled the whole earth, was never to have an end, "never to be destroyed." All the political empires that had ever existed before it had been destroyed by physical violence, but this one *was* not thus to be moved. The expression "The kingdom shall not be left to other people," implies that another people shall not overcome it; nor shall it even pass from one dynasty to another. Which is additional evidence to my mind that it is democratic. "The empire of the world, as we have seen in considering the first four empires, had passed from people to people, but, according to this the people of the fifth kingdom were to hold the scepter of empire perpetually. Other political powers were to be wholly removed," *no place was found for them*," "they became like chaff of the summer threshing floor, and the wind carried them away," but this empire stood up in everlasting continuance. It stood on earth: it stood where the Roman, the Grecian, the Persian, and the Assyrian empires stood, and there it *stood forever*. The judgment and the resurrection, and the regeneration of the heavens and earth by fire, did not move it, it shall stand and not be removed, forever. In its progress of glory, its territory may be cleansed by fire; its inhabitants may be purified by the judgment; the angels may "gather out of it all things that offend, and them that do iniquity," but the kingdom shall remain standing where it was originally established. It will be remembered, that the promise of perpetuity to the stone kingdom is precisely that made to Israel when restored to nationality in the latter day, of which, it is said, they shall never be removed but shall abide for ever and ever. Again, that the stone was a democratic government, is seen from the fact that it destroyed all monarchy. In the first chapter we remarked that there were only two kinds of governments; that there could be but two kinds from the constitution of man. One holds that the right of governing does not exist in the consent of the governed. The other holds that there is no right of government except by the expressed consent of the governed. And, my readers, it does not require the gift of prophecy, nor the gift to look into prophecy, to see that these two principles are antagonistic and that one *must* supplant the other in the earth; you believe, my dear reader, that the democratic principle will ultimately prevail. We affirm, that God unequivocally promises in his word, that it shall prevail. And in the vision which we are considering he teaches us that the day is coming when it shall sweep monarchy from the earth at a single dash. That little episode thrown in here, of which the Scriptures abound, where a few syllables express volumes, expresses much here. "Then was the iron, the clay, the brass, the silver and the gold, broken to pieces together, and became like the chaff of the summer threshing floors; and the wind carried them away, that no place was found for them."

Now, mark you, nothing of this kind was said when the Medo-Persian empire subverted the Babylonian or the Macedonian subverted the Medo-Persian, although they were utterly annihilated. Nothing has been known of them since; yet the Prophet uses no such language in reference to them, but as ever, the stone smites and destroys the Roman empire. The Prophet enumerates all that composed the political character of the whole entire image, "the iron, the clay, the brass," etc., and tells us "it became as chaff and the wind carried them away that no place was found for them." There will be no place found for monarchy in the regenerated earth and heavens. Dr. Baldwin says: "It is an undeniable fact that the great image represented all the human monarchy that was ever to be universal on earth. And it is also undeniable, that not one fragment of their political character was to remain, for " there was no place found for them." In the annihilation of these monarchies, it follows that the divine right of kings, claimed by them, was swept forever from the earth. Now, as the stone removed all of the political fabric of monarchy, and filled its place with another kind of government, it is evident that the government must be a republic, because it could be of no other kind. Again, no reason is assigned in the text for the hostility of the stone to the whole system of monarchy; yet it is plain that it purposed to break up and totally extirpate not one part only of the system of monarchy, but it was *terribly* hostile to the minutest fragment of it. This again indicates its republican character, for there is an innate hostility in republicanism to monarchy, nor can it ever rest satisfied while it sees a monarchy in existence. It is belligirent to the very name of a human king, and its highest indignation is never reached unless it is roused on account of monarchy. We have already shown that God hates monarchy and loves a theocratic democracy, such as that of republican Israel; and as he established the stone kingdom, it is evident that he would conform it to his notions of a true government, which is that of a democracy with himself as the chosen head. The fifth kingdom or government would, therefore, be a Christian democracy. The stone, it is observable, did not incorporate one particle of clay or of the metals with itself; it preserved its lithological nature, unmixed by any affinity with the political qualities of clay or metal; it must, therefore, have been a republic. But as God was its founder he must have been acknowledged as its head, so that it was just such a republic as that which entered Canaan under Joshua. Now we will see how the United States comports with the stone kingdom. As some may think the idea of the United States in prophecy a chimerical one, we will quote from Dr. Baldwin on the probability that the United States would be a theme of prophecy. "The rise of the United States," says he, "began the great era of national humanity in the world. Cruelty and blood had been the principal features in the governments, from Babylon down to the Declaration: and the Declaration enumerates a catalogue of abuses and cruelties, on the part of England, for which rebellion was the only remedy.

"The successful example of a rebellion on the part of oppressed subjects soon taught monarchies to lighten the pressure of their iron heel upon the necks of the crushed. Hence, the cessation of inquisitions, *auto de fes* and the general and bloody massacres of the good. The rise of the United States was the era of a nationality. Bad as many of our people are, our plague spots are purity compared to the corruptive courts of other lands."

"Never did a nation have such a feeling heart as ours. The cry of starving Ireland wakens no chord in the heart of the Lion and Unicorn, but it thrills the bosoms of our millions, and they give with a free and full hand to the fainting *slaves* of *British*

FREEDOM. The despairing cry of liberty from Hungary, stirs all, from ocean to ocean, and they nurse the moan upon the breast of memory, till the day of vengeance comes. They open wide their gates, and with outstretched arms invite the weary and heavy laden to tarry with them and be refreshed, and sharpen their sword till the hour to strike for the world's release. They say, "whosoever will, let him come;" they say to the starving, "we have bread enough and to spare;" they say to the poor, "come share our rich inheritance;" they say to the oppressed, "take shelter under the stars of our banner;" and, while millions crowd the way, they say, "there's room for millions more." Our kind hearted country is "the desire of all nations;" and to it the nations come.

"Our rising was the epoch of knowledge among men, the realization of the prediction, "that many should run to and fro, and knowledge should be increased." With us the press, that luminary of liberty, arose like a splendid sun from the deeps of chaos, and, through the rifted clouds, flashed a bewildering brightness on the unused eyes of the world. The press was chained before; now it is free. Unnumbered millions of books and printed truths, each year, and month, and day, like bars, and beams, and rays of 'massy light,' pour their fair splendors on the immortal mind, through all our hemisphere. Here burns 'the lamp of eternity' on every table of the rich, and in every cottage of the lowly, lighting the soul with the knowledge of its sublimity, and the luster of Christianized humanity. Here science and art have sowed seed of perennial fruit, to grow and blossom now, and ripen early in the approaching millennial summer. Like fountains of worth and beauty, schools are among the hills and vales, and everywhere; and all 'our children are taught of the Lord.' Our rise was the epoch of agriculture, commerce, manufactures, and trade. Land had been tilled from Adam, to be sure, but when an empire was at once put under tribute by improved modes of production, there was an epoch. Cotton rules the world; and cotton makes an era in the world's prosperity; and with us its culture fully began. Commerce was but a fishing smack before our union, now it is a navy on all the seas around the globe. Navigation then was a snail, now it is a tempest; then it was a galley with oars, now it is a palace driven with superhuman and invisible force; then it was toil, now an exquisite luxury. Then manufactories were mere crudities, now they darken and deafen kingdoms with smoke and roar. Then all were poor, now all are independent; then all was sluggish, now all is motion; then all was ignorance, now all is information; then a pillar of cloud led the world, but now a pillar of fire.

But again, our rise was the birth of organized and democratic liberty. For such an event the nations had groaned, but never hoped to see. Philosophy had pronounced it impossible, and kings had scouted it as an idle conceit; yet it is realized at last. Its country, like a throne, is seated above all lands, upon the highest region of the globe. Its temple, like itself, is new, and free, and glorious. Its dome is the great open sky, adorned by God's own fingers, and lighted by lamps of his own kindling; circled with a cornice of his own painting, and animated with clouds moved and gilded by his own skill; its floor is the great continent bordered by seas on either side; its altar is the nation's heart; its music is the cheerful voice of the myriads of the free; its worship is the praise of God; and there is no image of a God within its mountain walls, for the true God is there in spirit. Our nation was "a nation born to God in a day"—born on Independence day.

Upon the world the effects of our birth have been "life from the dead." Every part of the civilized world, and especially the religious world, has felt our existence as if we had been a universal galvanic battery. Our influence abroad cannot be expressed by volumes of words; it cannot be measured by a gage, nor be estimated by balances, nor computed by figures. Revolutions are stirred by it, and every throne trembles on account of it; kings feel it, and the people are inspired by it; religion brightens through it, and apostate papacy shrinks from its touch. Blot us from the world, with all the influence we have exerted upon it, directly or indirectly, and how dark the globe would be! Hell would celebrate the catastrophe, and monarchs would invite all hell to a feast of thanksgiving at an event so delightful to iniquity. Pope and pagan would leap to youth from decrepitude, and despotism would embrace them again in its loving and confraternal arms, and all would dance with delight over their common and dreaded foe. No country ever existed that, in so short a space, affected the world so much and did so much for the good of the cause of God and humanity; and yet ours is but the state of infancy. Now, then, we ask a question: How can it be, that all other nations affecting the cause of God and man, should be specifically and repeatedly predicted by prophets, and our country, which has done more good than all others be unmentioned by the prophets? The prophets mention the minutest facts, and the smallest countries and villages that affected God's ancient and his modern Israel; and how happens it that not a word is said of America? Egypt and Greece, Edom and Moab, and Tyre, and Damascus, and Sidon, and all the little towns of Asia Minor, and the Levant, come in for a share of notice, and all the mighty empires affecting the church are carefully enumerated; the divisions of the Roman empire were specially noticed, down to the end of them all, and yet no notice given of a Christian country that gives more comfort and relief to the Christians and the distressed than was ever given by all the world put together? How can it be possible that this country was left out of prophecy? How came it to be the alone proscribed nation in all the prophetic calendar? You may talk largely of reformations in Church and State, but no great and organic reformations were, or are, complete and free elsewhere. And can the greatest epoch, the brightest era in the history of Christianity, be unnoticed in the scriptures, while all others of minor note are emphasized with a will? Surely no. Right where the prophets place the rise of Israel; right where the stone, or fifth kingdom, was to appear; right at that appointed time our Christian country arose, and it must be the fifth predicted kingdom.

"The stone was to arise after Church and State union, and in the broken state of Rome. The United States arose and no other did arise in this period except such as grew out of the image, or some fragment of it. Again, the stone kingdom came out of Christianity the mountain, and therefore possessed the dual character so often specified by the prophets, and which is an essential element of civil government. Washington, in his farewell address, says, 'With slight shades of difference, you have the same religion, manners, habits, and political principles.' As the United States possesses the double nature of the Christian religion and a Christian civil government, it coincides with the double character of the stone. Again, it is indisputable that the United States government arose out of a Christian people, and that the constitution is essentially Christian, but not sectarian. It recognizes all the great virtues and customs of true Christianity, and in all our history, the God of history has been authoritatively proclaimed as the king, and the only king of our people. The Declaration, the Constitution, the State laws, the executive, the judiciary and the legislative powers of our country, have manifested uniformly and decidedly, that Christianity was the basis of our political structure. Our coin sparkles with the illumination of Christianity, "*In God we trust.*" Again, the stone was to possess a political structure and a tremendous martial power. The exhibition we made of martial power in the great civil war, perfectly astonished all Europe, and made crowned heads tremble on their thrones. Again, the stone kingdom arose external to the Roman empire; it was not within its limits, it came from afar and attacked it externally. Now the Roman empire limits embraced all of civilized Europe, Asia and Africa, or the whole of the old world; and by consequence the stone kingdom was to be in some portion of the new world or America. To this conclusion we are logically and inevitably coerced. The United States was erected external to the Roman empire, and is the only continent out of it where a great empire, sufficien to do this work, could arise. Again, the fifth empire was to be a republic, *so is the United States.* Again, the fifth empire was to break up the whole fabric of monarchy by war, and was then to annihilate the fragments. It must be remembered, that the image represented all of human monarchy that was ever to exist; and the image was smitten by the stone and literally swept from the earth. As the events here predicted have not transpired, of course no coincidence, by the fulfillment, can be affirmed between the fifth kingdom and any power whatever, but show me a man or woman of observation that does not see plainly that the day is rapidly approaching when republicanism and monarchy shall close for the final struggle. Sound philosophy teaches that we cannot avoid a collision with monarchy in general.

We are taught in this vision that the whole system of monarchy was destroyed in the earth. What will destroy it? One monarch will destroy another and subvert his kingdom, but he will only build up monarchy the stronger by so doing. What will *destroy* it, we ask? I know you reply in your own minds, REPUBLICANISM will yet give it its death blow; and it will deal the blow at such a point in the system that the whole fabric shall fall with a crash in hopeless ruin. We can not, if we would, avoid a collision with monarchy. Its antipathy to democracy grows daily more intense, as it is obliged to be more watchful of its interests. America, it regards as the great crater of melted lava, whose streams are reaching its hemisphere; and it would be a matter of intoxicating delight to it if we were out of the way; and this feeling would lead it to put us out of the way if it could. It views with surly jealousy all our sympathy for the restless democracy struggling beneath it; and it is fully aware, that to possess a steady throne, America must be disorganized. It is stated that, in view of these very things, a proposition to destroy the American republic was proposed in Russia as early as 1818. Since the origin and success of organized democracy in America, the liberal principle has accumulated and grown with unprecedented rapidity in Europe, until France has driven monarchy from her soil, and the nobility of England to-day are but ornamental figure-heads. The innate hostility between liberalism and monarchy will, from the very nature of the case, lead to exterminating hostility of one party or the other; both cannot exist together in the world on a large scale and be at peace. This collision with monarchy is more clearly foretold in succeeding descriptions of the fifth kingdom, and in all the predictions of Israel restored. The destruction of monarchy by Israel restored is fully predicted by Ezekiel in the destruction of Gog. Daniel also predicts it in the political judgment day of the ancient of days, and in the fall of the wilful king in Israel's country. John repeats the same thing in the sixth seal, in the reaping of the earth, and in the taking of the beast and prophet by the man on the white horse, etc. Again, the fifth kingdom was to spread over the whole earth, after the destruction of monarchy, of course no full coincidence can here be shown, as no fulfillment has been realized. But the capacity of our government for unlimited expansion is a quality inherent in its federative structure and representative policy. Its tendency is, also, to accumulate territorial power. This tendency, not arising from individual lust of power, cannot be mischievous, as when it springs from the monarchical power of aggrandizement. The tendency with us springs from a desire to fulfill a divine command; to fill the earth, to till it, and subdue or civilize and refine and bless it. The easy yoke and gentle burden of our government is desired by almost all people, in preference to the chains of anarchy and iron collar of oppression. Our doctrine is, that if the people wish a government, they should have it in spite of kings. And if any people wish to be annexed to us, they should have their wishes gratified in spite of the hellish despotisms that crush them. Again, the fifth empire was to be established by the God of heaven. This is what is meant by the stone being cut out without hands, and nothing more than this.

The prophet says, in his own interpretation, "the God of heaven shall set up a kingdom" "for as much as thou sawest that the stone was cut out without hands." This does not imply any miraculous power at all, but simply providential care in its origin and progress. All "the powers that be are ordained of God" as well as the fifth empire. Yet the language plainly conveys the notion that it would be one that God would approve. Now, when we remember that America was kept from the world till an intelligent Christian people were ready to occupy it; when we see it made use of as a Christian refuge, till millions of Christian people were ready to organize a government in it, and then remember the commitment of their cause to God universally as a people, and as a government their choice of God as king, their days of humiliation, fasting and prayer for civil and religious redemption, the conviction is irresistible, that God especially looked to the United States as a government peculiarly his own. The acts of congress were in the name of God, and at its first session it adjourned and on a solemn day of fasting and prayer, dedicated themselves and their country to God; and on that memorable day, the people pledged themselves to God and liberty. Individuals and families, churches and colonies, prayed to God to establish a Christian nation of freemen. For this all the people from Washington down, all humbly bowed themselves in prayer to God. As one has said, from Lexington to the victory tears flowed and prayers ascended in one universal, undying cry, all over the land, for the salvation of God. The bannered hosts inscribed upon their standards "*Nil desperandum Christo Duce*," "He that brought us over will help us through." "Our appeal is to heaven." The great declaration, "relying on Divine Providence we pledge our lives." When God had gone forth with our hosts and the war had closed and success had crowned our efforts, then said the noble Washington to congress, "I consider it an indispensable duty to close the last solemn act of my official life by commending the interests of our dearest country to the protection of Almighty God, and those who have the superintendence of them to His *holy keeping*." To whom the president of congress, in behalf of that body, replied, "We join you in commending the interests of our dearest country to the protection of *Almighty God*, beseeching Him to dispose the hearts and minds of its citizens to improve the opportunity afforded them of becoming a happy and respectable nation." Well might Mr. Baldwin say, in reference to the above, "Nothing in the valedictories of Moses or Joshua is replete with nobler or sincerer consecration to Jehovah. He adds, "the people of the United States in the Revolutionary war, abandoned human monarchy *forever*, and chose God for their king; and God accepted the office and set their feet upon a rock and established their goings and put a song of praise in their mouth and a two-edged sword in their hand."

Lastly: The fifth kingdom was furiously hostile to monarch . This we all know is exactly descriptive of the character of the United States. We detest the very name of king and have no sort of respect for royalty, human crowns and scepters. It will be seen that the United States coincides with every characteristic of which the fifth kingdom was to be possessed, down to the present time. The great and essential points which are given to identify it, are the time of its rise, the source from which it was to come, the political character, it was to possess, its locality outside the limits of monarchy, and its direct hostility to Roman monarchy. With all these great marks of identity the United States perfectly coincides; and as perfect coincidence of persons, events and objects, with prophecy; is a perfect fulfillment of prophecy, it follows that the United States is the fulfillment of the fifth kingdom predicted by Nebuchadnezzar's vision.

> "Land of the west! though passing brief
>   The record of thine age,
> Thou hast a name that darkens all
>   On history's wide page!
>
> "Let all the blasts of fame ring out—
>   Thine shall be loudest far;
> Let others boast their satellites,
>   Thou hast the Morning Star.
>
> "Thou hast a name whose characters
>   Of light shall ne'r depart;
> 'Tis stamped upon the dullest brain,
>   And warms the coldest heart;
>
> "A war-cry fit for any land,
>   Where freedom's to be won;
> Land of the west! it stands alone—
>   It is thy Washington."

Then how beautifully the patriotic Reid sings:

> "Oh! joy to the world! the hour is come,
>   When the nations to freedom awake,
> When the royalists stand agape and dumb,
>   And monarchs with terror shake;
> Over the wall of majesty
>   '*Upharsin*' is writ in words of fire,
> And the eyes of the bondsman, wherever they be,
>   Are lit with wild desire.
> Soon shall the thrones that blot the world,
>   Like the Orleans, into the dust be hurled,
> And the word roll on like a hurricane's breath,
>   Till the furtherest slave hears what it saith—
> *Arise! arise!! Be free! be free!!*"

CHAPTER V.

Mr. Baldwin says: "One remarkable peculiarity of prophecy is, that every very important prophetic event is repeated twice, or twice doubled, and that the symbolic prophecies are mostly accompanied additionally with an interpretation. This principle is especially exhibited in the universal prophecies of the political world, recorded by Daniel. The vision we are about to consider, goes over the very same field of the one we have just left. When Joseph interpreted Pharoah's double vision of the seven fat and seven lean kine, and the seven full and seven blasted ears, he says: "For that the dream was doubled unto Pharoah twice, it is because the thing is established *by God* and God will shortly bring it to pass." We are told by this Scripture that the symbolic prophecies are doubled because the thing is *established*, and established *by God.* So we see by this that God emphasizes the *certain* fulfillment of the symbolic prophecies by repeating them.

This vision which is the second panorama of the six empires, is recorded in the seventh chapter of Daniel. It is prefaced with a prophetic introduction, which shows the entire compass of the prophecy. Daniel says: "I saw in my vision, and behold the four winds of heaven strove upon the great sea, and four great beasts came up from the sea, diverse from one another." The term seas in the prophecies symbolizes people, generally all the people of the world. I would refer you to Zech. 10-11; Hab. 3-8; and Rev. 7-3; where this signification is apparent. In this vision it also has this meaning. Daniel tells us in his interpretation that the four great beasts are four kingdoms, or four kings, and Hebrew scholars tell us that the original text could have been as properly rendered kingdoms. The two terms are interchangeable in the prophecies, and in fact, in common parlance, one implies the other.

These four empires arose in different ages of the world, and it is plain that the term sea embraces the whole world during their history, or the history of the people. The striving of the winds upon the sea represents commotions in the political world, and the striving of the *four* winds represents the universality of these changes and agitations. Jeremiah explains the term "four winds." He says in forty-ninth chapter and thirty-eighth verse: "I will bring against Elam four winds, from the four extremities of the heavens." After this brief prophetic introduction, in which Daniel saw the commotion in the elements, which symbolized the commotions in the political world, or birth throes which preceded the rise of these great empires, he goes immediately on to describe the appearance of the four beasts, which illustrates the political character of the first four empires of the monarchy image, which we have just been considering. The Prophet says: "The first was like a lion, and had eagle's wings; I beheld until the wings thereof were plucked and it was lifted up from the earth and made to stand upon the feet as a man, and a man's heart was given to it."

We have not space nor time to give a detailed list of the points of coincidence, nor is it necessary; we have just been over the four kingdoms, and spoken of their characteristics, and you have read of them in history; when we speak of the more prominent points of coincidence you can easily run them out in your own mind. This beast was a lion. A lion fitly represents the Babylonian empire. Jeremiah describes it as a lion in the 4th chapter, 6th verse, "the lion is come up from his thicket, and the destroyer of the Gentiles is on his way;" this lion had wings. Ezekiel said of Babylon, "he shall fly as an eagle and shall spread his wings over Moab." In the 17th chapter he calls it "a great eagle with great wings." It being "lifted up from the earth and made to stand upon the feet as a man and a man's heart given to it," shows a change of character in the government, from a beastly to a human character, after the king's conversion. These characteristics are agreed to by all writers, as identifying the winged lion with the first of the four great empires. Again, "and behold another beast, a second, like unto a bear, and it raised itself on one side; and it had three ribs in the mouth of it, between the teeth of it; and they said unto it arise, devour much flesh." This beast represents the second kingdom in the series of the four. The Medo-Persian was the second universal empire in the series of universal empires of the world. Again, it raised itself on one side; the double dynasty of Medes and Persians coincides with the two sides of the bear; and the final superiority and ascendency of the Persians over the Medes, coincides with the raising of one side of the bear. Again, the three ribs in the mouth of the bear, finds their coincidence in the three vice-royalties into which the empire was divided, and of which Daniel speaks. He says, "it pleased Darius to set over the kingdom a hundred and twenty princes, which should be over the whole kingdom, and over these three presidents. Again, the conquests of the Medes and Persians were very extensive, and very cruel and destructive, and in this respect they jointly coincide with the "devouring of much flesh." Again, "After this I beheld, and lo! another like a leopard, which had upon the back of it four wings of a fowl; the beast had also four heads, and dominion was given to it." This was the third beast, and it represented the third universal kingdom, which was the Macedonian. The four corners of the earth signify also the four wings of the earth, and wings signify powers or governments and also velocity. The leopard being a spotted beast, represents a mottled or mixed kingdom The leopard had four heads. Of course the kingdom was to be divided into four parts. This, with the four wings, is a double indication of the quadruple character the kingdom was to exhibit. We learn in the Apocalypse that a head signifies a kind of government. With these characteristics, you can see at a glance how perfectly the Macedonian empire agrees.

Again: "After this I saw in the night vision, and behold a fourth beast, dreadful and terrible, and strong exceedingly, and it had great iron teeth; it devoured and broke in piece, and stamped the residue with the feet of it, and it was diverse from all the beasts that were before it, and it had ten horns." When Daniel asked the angel to interpret this for him. "Thus, he said, the fourth beast shall be the fourth kingdom upon the earth, which shall be diverse from all the kingdoms, and shall devour the whole earth, and shall tread it down and break it in pieces." The points of character to identify it in this period of its history are (1) It was to be the fourth universal empire; (2) it was to be exceeding powerful above all nations before it, (3) it was to differ from all the other kingdoms; (4) it was to subdue the whole earth by violence; (5) its political complexion was to be of iron teeth and nails of brass. With these characteristics the Roman empire fully coincides. It was the fourth great kingdom. It was the most powerful nation that ever existed. It differed from all the great kingdoms before it in almost every great point of excellence. It subdued all nations, and made them tributary to its power. Its political complexion was Roman and Grecian, or iron and brass; the destroying policy is here represented by iron teeth, as it was represented by iron in Nebuchadnezzar's vision. Again the Prophet says, "I considered the horns and behold there came up behind (Mede Faber, &c.) them another little horn before whom there were three of the first horns plucked up by the roots, and behold in this horn were eyes like the eyes of a man, and a mouth speaking great things." Then Daniel again applies to his celestial interpreter, and says, "I would know the truth of the fourth beast, and of the ten horns that were in his head, and of the other horn which came up, and before whom three fell, even of that horn that had eyes, and a mouth that spake very great things, whose look was more stout than his fellows," and the angel replied, "The ten horns out of this kingdom are ten kings (or kingdoms) that shall arise, and another shall arise behind them, and he shall be diverse from the first, and shall subdue three kings, and he shall speak great words against the Most High, and shall wear out the saints of the Most High, and think to change times and laws, and they shall be given into his hand, until a time, and times, and the dividing of a time. But the judgment shall sit, and they shall take away his dominion to consume and destroy it unto the end." Now, we know that the body of the fourth beast represents the fourth kingdom in a united state, for so the Prophet says, this state of the kingdom was represented in the other vision by the iron alone before the clay came in. The divided state of the fourth kingdom there represented by ten toes is here represented by the ten horns; for the Prophet says the ten horns are ten kings or kingdoms. The number ten was a representative number, and simply implied that the empire should be so effectually broken up that ten separate kingdoms should be formed out of it, though many more in time should appear. In looking into this vision we see the union of Church and State, which was represented in the other vision by the coming in of the clay with the iron, here represented with astonishing clearness by the rise of the little horn.

I will not occupy further space here to give all the coincidences between this little horn kingdom and the papal power, you can easily run them out in your own mind. Messrs. Mede, and Faber, and others, in their translations tell us that this horn arose anterior to the ten, and before the divided stat of the Roman empire, at the very time of Church and State union. This little horn was to differ in political nature from the other horns. "He shall be diverse from the first." It was to be a spiritual power as well as political. "Behold in this horn were eyes like the eyes of a man, and a mouth speaking great things; his look was more stout than his fellows,' etc. It was to speak great things and great words against the

Most High, and the saints were to be given into its hand. From this special oversight of the saints, and its political character diverse from the other powers, and its eyes and mouth of a prophet, directing words against God, it is evident that this horn was principally a spiritual power, though blended with the political as is indicated by the union of the two eyes in the horn or head. He was to "think, to change times and laws;" this is plainly expressive of a will on his part, to change political or spiritual policy, or both. You can compare these things in your own mind with the past history of the papal power. The fact of the horn being a spiritual power, inclines us to the opinion that the laws and times given to it were of a spiritual nature, rather than political. Again, it was to "wear out the saints." The term saints—as we have seen—in the Old Testament is synonymous with Christian in the New. It is remarkable that in all of Daniel's prophecies of the latter day, he never mentions the name of Israel or Judah, or anything about Jews after the destruction of Jerusalem. The wearing out of the saints implies a general persecuted condition, hence, the little horn was a persecuting ecclesiastical power. The Prophet then adds: "I beheld till the thrones were cast down." This expression synchronizes with the destruction of monarchy by the stone kingdom in the other vision, and relates to the same time and event, and then he immediately adds, "and the Ancient of days did sit." Now here, we are aware we must meet with settled prejudice. It is natural for those who do not make the prophecies a particular study, and hence are wholly unacquainted with the conventional rules of interpretation, to interpret the prophecies, and especially the symbolic prophecies, according to the apparent construction of the language, making part literal and part symbolical. A great many, in this passage, have been in the habit of referring the expression, *Ancient of days*, to *God*. But this is a symbolic character like all the rest, and means Israel restored. One like the Son of Man came with the clouds of heaven, and he came to the Ancient of days. Christ went to God; is now with him. Here, we are told, he comes from God and comes to the Ancient of days, and *they*—not the Ancient of days, nor God—but THEY (pronoun of multitude), the people of the Ancient of days, brought him near and the kingdom was given to him. We have the best authority that a man, as a symbol, always represents a government of some kind. Thus Judah is put for the Jewish nation, so also is Israel and Ephraim and Jacob. The great image of Nebuchadnezzar's vision also represents a body of government, and so also does the "Man of Sin." The two horned beast, or false prophet, in the book of Revelation, also symbolizes a nation So also a woman is put for an ecclesiastical body of government, and in general a human person represents any organized body of power. The throne on which he sits symbolizes a government or organized body of people. In the symbolic prophecies every word is fraught with the greatest and most important meaning. Kingdom and throne are used synonymous in the prophecies. Pharaoh says to Joseph, "only in the throne will I be greater than thou." We have seen that this symbolic personage sitting upon the throne represented a body of the people that had been an organization in ancient days, but now are restored, for the "Son of Man" comes to it, as he was to come to Israel restored, and it says here that "there was given him dominion, and glory, and a kingdom, that all people, nations, and languages, should serve him; his dominion is an everlasting dominion, which shall not pass away, and his kingdom that which shall not be destroyed." If this is not the Israel restored, which the prophets dwell upon so much, it can never be restored, for here is the same endless perpetuity and universality of empire and dominion that is always predicted of Israel restored, and is said and can be said, of no other nationality. The Prophet is not speaking here of the rise of Israel restored; he does speak of its rise, you will see, in the twenty-first and twenty-second verses, where he says: "I beheld, and the same horn made war with the saints, and prevailed against them, until the Ancient of days *came;*" not *did sit,* but came; "and judgment was given to the saints of the Most High, and the time came that the saints possessed the kingdom."

The judgment which Daniel speaks of here in the tenth verse is a political judgment, but reads so much like the spiritual judgment recorded in St. John in the 20th chapter of Revelation, that the casual reader blends the two. The 22d verse of this prophecy, that we are considering, tells us that this judgment was given into the hands of the saints, but the spiritual judgment of St. John is given into no hands but those of the Eternal Judge. One is at the ushering in of the millennium, the other (the spiritual) is at the close of that period. But after its rise the prophet continued to look prospectively into the future, for he says, "I beheld *till,*" &c. He saw the Son of Man come and take the government.

Now, there is nothing plainer than that Christ's second coming is a literal personal coming, just as certain as Christ was once on earth *in person,* just so certainly has he promised to come again *in person.* Both at the hour of his ascension, and at other times, has he promised it. We can only touch on these points here. We will treat of them more at length in another treatise. And it is equally plain that when he comes he is coming, to his Ancient of days, or to his own nationality of ancient days, restored in a Christian dress, or, in other words, Christ is coming to sit upon the throne of Israel restored to nationality.

Mr. Baldwin says of the Ancient of days, "The name of the ancient of days implies its priority of existence, as a nationality in kind, it had ceased to exist, but now rises into being again, indeed the very coming of the ancient implies his absence from a position he once occupied. As it was in a Christian dress, it is evident that it must have existed previously in a different style. As there was no democracy in olden times, with which the ancient could be compared, except the Hebrew republic of ancient days, it is clear that the allusion is to that, and as the restoration of Israel to nationality in the latter day was promised, and as that nationality was to be a Christian one, it is conclusive that the Ancient of days was the promised nationality of Israel restored—the democracy of Israel in a Christian dress." That the "Ancient of days symbolized an organized nationality of people possessing an overwhelming martial power is evident from the fact that the vision represents the ancient of days so destroying Roman Europe, this is a clear case. It also represents him as giving the kingdom to the Son of Man, after he had taken it. Now, the interpretation says, the saints shall take the kingdom, and the people of the saints shall possess it; the saints and the people of the saints are represented as synonymous with the throne and the ancient upon it. Again, the vision emphatically shows that these people of saints existed in a terrible and glorious organization, for all of the imagery representing them is most vividly organic.

Again, the thousand thousands that ministered to the ancient, shows that an organic mass of people were united to execute one single design. But farther still, the work which the ancient had on hand, shows that he represents a nationality. His work was to destroy a mighty empire; to overthrow Europe; to cast down thrones; to sit in judgment on over a hundred millions of people and to annihilate the empire church, as well as the Roman state of Europe. Such a work necessitates him to be a political fabric as well as a spiritual one.

Now the prophet tells us plainly that church and state union should prevail, should practice and prosper, for a certain time. He says " and he shall speak great words against the Most High, and shall wear out the saints of the Most High, and think to change times and laws: they shall be given into his hand until a time and times and the dividing of time." Mr. Baldwin has reckoned this time with great care, and on it he says as follows: "The truth of the whole matter of the papal power in Europe is this; the church was united to the State in the year 325 A. D. on the 19th of June. We place church and State union on the opening day of the council of Nice, because it was on that day that the first great ecclesiastical assembly met by order of the imperial decree and in the morning the emperor appeared in the assembly and in an oration proclaimed formally the powers he conferred upon them in the State. He stated, impliedly, that the decision of that assembly should be respected as law in the empire by imperial sanction; and from that day to this that speech he made has been the understood basis of church and State union. He proposed to settle church differences, and enforce church unity of faith, hoping, (says he) by my interference, a remedy might be applied to the evil, I sent for you all without delay—The various decrees of that beginning of iniquitous councils, were sanctioned by imperial authority, and on the first day of the council was formally begun a system of ecclesiastical despotism under which millions have suffered martyrdom. It was the first formal meeting of civil and ecclesiastical power in union." Mr. Baldwin makes the three and one-half times to be equal to 529,984 days, and then he adds, "if we date the origin of the papal power on the 19th of June 325 A. D., the day of the session of the council of Nice, and its opening by the emperor, and then add to it 529,984 days it brings us down exactly to the 4th day of July, 1776. On that very day the United States declared their independence of civil and ecclesiastical monarchy, and that day was the first on which the church had been freed from the domination of civil and ecclesiastical power from the days of Constantine." At that time the wearing out of the saints, the persecution of Rome ceased. At that time a nation was born in a day.

CHAPTER VI.

There are some things so unequivocally predicted in Scripture that no one can dispute them. Men may refuse to believe that the predictions will ever be fulfilled, and believers may differ as to the manner in which they will be fulfilled, but as to the fact of their being predicted in the sacred record, none will deny. Some of those things are the following: The restoration of God's Israel to nationality; that that nationality will destroy all the kingdoms of this world, and will extend itself over the entire globe; that it will endure forever; that in destroying the kingdoms of this world it is to do it in one grand battle called the battle of "Armageddon;" that this great battle ushers in the millenial period; that Christ is to make a second advent to earth, when He is to take the reins of government in His own nationality, or in Israel restored, and is to reign forever and ever, and that He is to come at the millennial period; that the millenial period is stated in Scripture to be 1000 years, at the close of which a second Armageddon battle is fought, in which all that opposeth itself to God, in all his vast empire, is destroyed. The last Armageddon is the closing up of the millennial period and the perfection and consummation of all things, beyond which we have no revelation. The last Armageddon is recorded but once in Scripture. The first one is constantly the subject of prophetic prediction throughout the sacred volume.

It is suggested in the following, and all similar passages (Isa. 66–16), "For behold the Lord will come with fire and with his chariot like a whirlwind, to render his anger with fury and his rebuke with flames of fire. For by fire and by his sword will the Lord plead with all flesh, and the slain of the Lord shall be many." And at the close of Daniel's fourth vision, in speaking of the invasion of monarchy, he says, "He shall plant the tabernacle of his palace between the seas in the glorious holy mountain yet he shall come to his end and none shall help him." It is recorded in Revelation, in the symbolic language, where Michael and his angels fought with the dragon and his angels, and after the victory "there were great voices in heaven, saying. The kingdoms of this world are become the kingdoms of our Lord, and of his Christ, and he shall reign for ever and ever.

Mr. Baldwin thinks the battle is to be fought in the United States, and as it is to be in a great valley, he places it in the valley of the Mississippi. But we must say, notwithstanding we have such authority as Dr. Baldwin against us, we think it will be fought in Europe. Dr. Baldwin cites the Scriptures where it says, referring to the leader of the forces of monarchy, " He shall fall on the mountains (State governments) of Israel." Again, "He shall plant the tabernacles of his palaces and come to his end, in the glorious holy mountain (nationality) between the seas," &c.

We claim that in that day—which we believe is not very far distant—there will be several republican States in Europe confederate with us, and as all the forces of the monarchy are there, they will march over onto the mountains of Israel (State governments of Israel) in Europe, and plant his tabernacle in the glorious holy mountains (nationalities) and come to his end between the two seas."

Immediately after this great king-destroying battle, Christ appears the second time on earth. Now, as to the manner of his coming, whether a personal or spiritual coming, which is tantamount to saying a real or visionary appearing, there are differences of opinion. Some seem to think that a personal appearing of Christ, belittles the great event, of this second coming; but whoever reads this treatise will have quite the opposite opinion, we think. Nothing could so gloriously magnify and clothe with grandeur the stupendous event of God's peopling this planet; His establishing his kingdom here after the fall of man; the war He inaugurated against rebellion; the conquest of the world by Christ himself; the overthrow of Satan and the powers of darkness; the recovery of the world to purity and good government; we say that nothing could so clothe it with grandeur and dignity and divine glory as Christ's triumphal return to it after the final victory. He is not coming alone, as he did the first time he came; as it were, stealing his way back; "He is coming with ten thousand of his saints." The New Jerusalem descends "from God out of heaven," and makes the place of his feet glorious; then Christ comes with the hosts (clouds) of heaven, the millions of His redeemed. It is the great coronation day, when Christ takes the kingdom to reign forever as Lord of lords and King of kings. "Hallelujah! Glory to God in the highest! Shout, angels, shout, and loudest ye redeemed." We hold that when Christ said he was coming again, that he meant as he had once come in personal reality; so he was in reality coming in person again. We believe this is what the angels meant that stood by at His ascension and said to his wrapt disciples as they gazed after him. "Ye men of Galilee, why stand ye gazing up into heaven? This same Jesus, which is taken up from you into heaven, shall so come in *like manner* as ye have seen him go into heaven." And in 24th chapter of Matthew, he cautions us not to be deceived on this point. He says if any man shall say unto you, that he has come; "Lo, here is Christ, or there, believe him not." Should they say, "behold he is in the desert, go not forth, behold he is in the secret chamber, believe it not; for as the lightning cometh out of the east and shineth even unto the west, so shall also the coming of the Son of Man be." He is not speaking here of the Spirit. When he left us he said he would send us the Spirit, and he should testify of him, and should remain with us until he *comes again*, and the Spirit did come on the day of Pentecost, and is with us to-day as every Christian can testify; but here he is speaking of personal identity, and adds the figurative language, wherever the carcass is there will the eagles be gathered together," and again, "every eye shall see him," &c.

There is equally as much difference of opinion in reference to the period of his advent, whether during the millennium, or at its close, or at the beginning. We hold that He comes soon after the great battle of Armageddon and his coming ushers in the millennium. We think Daniel puts his coming at this point of time. He says, "I beheld till the thrones were cast down." He continues to look into the future until he saw the great battle of Armageddon fought: Saw the nationality of Christian Israel destroy monarchy: Saw the present system of self-government, the present organization of democracy in the earth hurl the thrones into the dust. And then he immediately saw one like the Son of Man come to Israel restored and they gave him the kingdom. And he goes immediately on and describes it as the millennial kingdom. He says, "that all people, nations, and languages should serve him; his dominion is an everlasting dominion which shall not pass away, and his kingdom that which shall not be destroyed." If this is not the millennial kingdom, it crowds the millennial kingdom out of the earth, for it is universal and endures for ever and ever, and Christ comes at its introduction. And again, in the 20th chapter of Revelation you will find the millennial period is stated to be just one thousand years in duration, and those that are His are to be there and are expressly said to reign with Christ a thousand years of millennial reign, which they could not do if Christ was not there at the ushering in of the millennium. Again, "immediately after the tribulation of those days, shall the sun be darkened, and the moon shall not give her light, and the stars shall fall from heaven, and the powers of the heaven shall be shaken, and then shall appear the sign of the Son of Man in heaven, and then shall all the tribes of the earth mourn, and they shall see the Son of Man coming in the clouds of heaven with power and great glory." It is hardly necessary to say that this language is symbolical for notwithstanding our grandmothers have taught us that the meteoric shower a number of years since, was the falling of the stars in fulfillment of the prediction of Christ, yet there are none of us but what know that if one of those bright luminaries that we see sparkling in the far off fields of space were to fall upon this planet, it would bury us almost below resurrection power, for some of them are many thousand times larger than this earth.

But this language is not so poor as that, it has a richness and a grandeur, and a sublimity that belongs to the symbolic language of scripture. Heaven, as a symbol, means the place of the church on earth, and earth, as a symbol, means the place of the state or the civil power. The sun symbolizes the state or civil power, and the moon symbolizes the church. A star, almost invariably, symbolizes a prince or ruler; as Balaam says, "there shall come a *star* out of Jacob and a scepter shall arise out of Israel."

Hebrew poetry where one line explains the foregoing. Our Savior in the text quoted, is speaking of the battle of Armageddon, the destruction of monarchy and his own speedy coming, he says, "after the tribulations of those days the sun shall be darkened," there shall be trouble in the State, national darkness, political troubles, not in the United States, but in the monarchical or false government, those that are to be overthrown. "The moon shall not give her light." The established Churches, Church and State union, the Church shall not give her light; "and the stars shall fall," the princes or rulers shall fall at the fall of monarchy. Daniel says, "I beheld till the thrones were cast down," "and the powers of the heavens shall be shaken." All established churches shall be shaken down together with monarchy, but many of their members shall be saved, and then he adds, "and then shall appear the sign of the Son of Man in heaven." This heaven is symbolic and means the place of the church, the sign shall be here, and all the tribes of the earth shall mourn when they see the sign; and then they shall "see the Son of Man coming in the clouds of heaven with power and great glory." As soon as monarchy is destroyed; as soon as the "stars fall," that is, the princes and their thrones are cast down; as soon as the great battle of Armageddon is fought. The bright and morning star is seen in the heavens, and a light bursts from the East—the place of light—and streams athwart the heavens, for the sun that set in blood on Calvary has arisen to set no more. The desire of nations has come at last; but O how unlike his first coming; he comes no more the babe of Bethlehem cradled in a manger, clinging to the bosom of his outcast mother. No more pursued in his helpless infancy by the inhuman Herod; no more the unassuming man, traveling about Judea on foot, with his plain attire and seamless coat; no more dragged about by the Jerusalem mob, buffeted, spit upon, scourged and crucified. Now he comes wearing the livery of heaven, and upon his vesture is a name, " Lord of Lords, and King of Kings." He says he comes "with the clouds of heaven." If this is symbolic, a cloud symbolizes a vast concourse of people as "a great cloud of witnesses." Think you not he is coming as Moses said he should come, "with ten thousand of his saints," and his legion of angels? Are not these the clouds of heaven that he is coming with? What think you? I cast my eye back to the days of his humiliation, and I see him approaching Jerusalem "meek and riding upon an ass," a great throng follows him and they spread their garments in the way before him, and "they that went before and they that followed, cried, saying, hosanna to the son of David, blessed is he that cometh in the name of the Lord, blessed be the kingdom of our father David, that cometh in the name of the Lord, hosanna in the highest." His persecutors and enemies say, behold the whole world has gone after him. No, not the whole world at that time, but I cast a prophetic eye into the future and I see him approaching the gates of the New Jerusalem with a shining retinue; it is a vast throng, a great cloud, no man can number them. The earth is yet damp and red with the blood of slaughtered enemies; the great battle of Armageddon is fought, and the triumphant host approaches the gates of pearl, and we hear a voice from the vast multitude like the sound of many waters saying, "lift up your heads, O ye gates, and be ye lifted up ye everlasting doors, and the King of Glory shall come in." Then the cautious sentinel (cautious, because of the recent invasion) answers, "who is this King of Glory?" Then the multitude replies again, "the Lord strong and mighty, the Lord mighty in battle; lift up your heads, O ye gates, even lift them up ye everlasting doors, and the King of Glory shall come in." The cautious sentinel once more asks "who is this King of Glory?" Then the multitude again shouts, "the Lord of hosts, he is the King of Glory." The doors fly up and the pearly gates swing wide, and the Lord of hosts and his cloud of saints enter.

"Now see!
'Tis come, the glorious morn; the second birth
Of heaven and earth! Awakening nature hears
The new creating word, and starts to life,
In every brightened form, from pain and death
Forever free!"

We believe his triumphant entry into old Jerusalem, was a type of his glorious entry into the New Jerusalem. The lamb smoking on Jewish altar, never found its antetype in the Lamb of God on Calvary more completely than will that rejoicing throng—though a faint representation of it—find its antetype in His glorious Godlike approach to Christian Israel's nationality on coronation day. This is glorious to contemplate; more glorious to behold its realization. But, my dear reader, we are to be there in person, we are to help swell the vast ranks of the King of Glory as they enter in through the pearly gates; pass under the triumphal arches; pass through the gold-paved city; behold her bulwarks; see the King in his beauty; walk out under the regenerated heavens; set these feet upon the regenerated earth, and breathe, for the first time, the pure untainted atmosphere of mellinnial perfection. But, alas! Are there any who shall be cast off as unworthy to share in these glories? Yes; there are some who are "aliens to the commonwealth of Israel and strangers to the covenant of promise." God grant, that our readers may be found there and enter in through the gates into the city, and "behold the King in His beauty," for "without are dogs, and sorcerers, and whoremongers, and murderers, and idolaters, and whosoever loveth and maketh a lie." We might here speak of the probable nearness of these events to our day. We do not propose to prophesy, for we are not a prophet, but the world is becoming very expectant, as they were just before His first appearance on earth, If any one can tell me when those signs of which Christ speaks in the 24th chapter of Matthew, when they begin, when the first one appears; we can tell you within a very few years when Christ will appear, for he there says, they shall transpire in rapid succession, and all be accomplished, together with his coming, in one generation. It is a peculiarity of the Scriptures, that the inspired writer in narrating chronological events, uses the present tense. When Daniel gave the history of kingdom after kingdom, until he had reached the broken or divided state of Rome, in the remote future 2,500 years from his own day, then as he prophetically stood in that far distant age, and surveyed the political world, and saw many kings reigning in their respective kingdoms, he says, "in the days of *these* kings," &c. You see he uses the present tense. So our Savior, when he had related sign after sign, which preceded his second coming, then says, "Verily I say unto you, this generation shall not pass, till all these things be fulfilled; heaven and earth shall pass away, but my words shall not pass away."

In our next treatise we shall take up the wonderful symbolic prophecies of the Book of Revelation; that wonderful prophetic imagery, which to one who has no key to them, sounds like the bombastical ravings of a maniac. But to one who comprehends the prophetic theme, and can see the application of his God-like symbols, it is the grandest, the most beautiful, the most sublime imagery ever thrown upon the mental canvas.

In taking up the Revelations, when speaking of the sixth and seventh trumpet periods, we shall have occasion to speak more particularly of the signs preceding his coming, and in what age of the prophetic history we are living. We are doubtless not far from those great political events which immediately preceded the millennium. Christ labors hard to impress us with the fact, that when we see the signs which he has just been speaking of, the events just preceding and following the great battle of Armageddon, that it is near at hand, he says, "now learn a parable of the fig tree; when his branch is yet tender, and putteth forth leaves, we know that summer is at hand." Then he adds, "So likewise, ye, when ye shall see all these things, know that it is near, even at the doors."

> "He comes! He comes! the Judge severe!
> The seventh trumpet speaks him near."

> "From heaven angelic voices sound;
> See the Almighty Jesus crown'd!
> Girt with omnipotence and grace,
> And glory decks the Saviour's face."

> "Then He descending on His throne,
> Shall claim the kingdoms for His own;
> The kingdoms all obey His word,
> And hail Him their triumphant Lord."

> "Shout, all the people of the sky;
> And all the saints of the Most High;
> Our Lord, who now His right obtains,
> *Forever* and FOREVER reigns."

THE SEQUELA.

GOD'S PURPOSES IN THE MATERIAL UNIVERSE AND THE REASON OF WORLDS.

It is apparent to every thinking mind, that all of the material universe had a beginning; and, also, there was a time when each and every finite intelligence, whether in heaven or in earth, began their being. Hence, in carrying out this course of reasoning, we find that there was a time in the eternity past —however remote—when God was alone in the universe, or so to speak, when God and space were absolute. There was not an intelligent being to hymn his praises, or enjoy his goodness. No seraph's wing fanned the eternal throne. No angelic hosts saluted the ear of Jehovah with their hallelujahs. No blood-washed throng of redeemed spirits encircled his throne filling the vaults of heaven with the song of redemption.

Not a blazing sun with its fiery track; not a star looked down from the empyrean heights. Not a teeming world rolled in the voids immense. All was silence! All was God! No intelligent beings to sing his praise or reciprocate his love and goodness. And no forces had as yet gone out from him commissioned to form the material universe. But God is infinite goodness. If there is one of His perfections that shines brighter than another, it is His goodness. The Bible seems to put considerable stress on this perfection, the goodness of God.

When Moses asked to behold his person, he says: "I will make all my *goodness* pass before thee"—as though he had displayed all the glory of his person when he had displayed all his goodness. And as He passed before Moses He proclaimed, "The Lord, the Lord God, merciful and gracious, long suffering and abundant in *goodness* and truth." Now it is the chief characteristic of goodness to diffuse itself. It ignores all selfishness. It is benevolence and love embodied and alive, full of plans for the benefit of others, and must be actively at work to make them effective. Its expansive nature will not let it rest in itself. It must have objects upon which to act; sentient, intelligent beings that can appreciate and reciprocate this goodness and bring some return to God in praise and adoration. Hence, we behold another period in the annals of eternity past when God first sent forth the creative fiat, and those pure spirits, the angelic hosts, circled around his throne with harps and voice attuned to his praise.

And when we say they were created from a spark of his own intelligence, we will doubtless meet with no opposition, not even a severe criticism. But when we come to speak of the material universe originating in an analogous way, we may hear the cry of materialism, or worse if possible. But as we have good company both in the scientific and theological world, we shall fearlessly proceed.

And in pursuing the subject we come to another period, when God purposed to fill this space infinite with beautiful worlds and flaming suns. Not simply and alone to display to these intelligent angelic beings which he had created, his power and wisdom, and goodness, and perfection of beauty, etc. Though we are told that these angelic beings, "the sons of the morning" of creation, shouted together and encircled Jehhvah's throne with a volume of praise as they saw these beautiful worlds forming, for, "The first archangel never saw so much of God before." And the Psalmist could truthfully sing, "The heavens declare the glory of God and the firmament sheweth his handiwork," etc. And they do in very deed, proclaim with thousand tongues to all his creatures the existence of that God tha. formed them, and reflect his glory.

"Forever singing as they shine,
The hand that formed us is Divine."

But it was not for this purpose that he made the worlds, it was on a higher and broader and more noble plan, a plan that becomes the dignity of a God. It was to people them with intelligent life; not in the condition we find ourselves here on this planet, sin-cursed in open rebellion against him, a world of sin, sorrow and suffering and all the wretchedness that sin brings upon intelligent moral beings, this was not his original purpose, his plans have been broken in upon by an enemy, *but not defeated* as you shall know before we are done with the subject. But the question arises and should be considered here before we go further, how did he create the world?

As some think they see a discrepancy between science and the cosmagony of Moses recorded in Genesis. We would remark here that we have nothing to do with the wild hypothesis of some of our scientists but only with true science, and all *true* science throws light upon God's revelation and aids greatly in its interpretation, and Bishop Warren, has shown conclusively that God's revelation aids materially in the discoveries of science.

Now when we come to consider the manner in which God formed the worlds, and is forming them for the same forces are operating now that have been operating in the past, we find that science teaches us that all things are from a gaseous state. That this is so is apparent on every hand. If man by a chemical process can turn solids to a liquid and from a liquid to a gaseous condition and from a gaseous back to a solid, it is proof that the great Alchemist of the universe has done so and still works in that way. Take for instance your quicksilver, put it into your crucible kindle the fire under it and it will pass into the atmosphere in the form of gas, let that gas as it rises from the crucible pass through a pipe, insert the end of the pipe in cold water and you will throw it back into a liquid state, then take it to Montreal or Alaska in the dead of winter and you can pound it out like lead or silver in a solid state

Water is said to be a mineral because it will pass from a solid to a gaseous under such a low pressure, and the freezing point solidifies. But this fact was most forcibly illustrated in the lixiviation process, by which they worked their ores in the reduction works at the "Silver King" mine in Arizona, by which process they threw the metal in those ores into a liquid state. We do not understand the processes, but we saw the result, —it ran off from the tubs in the water, clear and beautiful, as limpid as the water of a mountain spring. By their chemical processes they brought it to a plastic state, about the consistency of soft dough or putty, they then put it in an oven to harden. There some of the silver was doubtless lost by being thrown into a gaseous state by the heat, as is proven by the fact that gas escaping around the iron doors, and through the cracks in the furnace, the silver would form as it came in contact with the air, in the peculiar formations in which we find it in its original deposits in the mines. No one has been able to explain why it always takes those peculiar forms, not even Mr. Tilden; we mean the beautiful fern formation and peculiar wire formation, &c. They were finally compelled to give up the lixiviation processes. The character of the ores so changed as they went deeper into the mine, that in passing through the roasters the mineral was thrown into a gaseous state, and passed off into the atmosphere through the smoke-pipes, and the mineralogist told us that with pipe *enough* he could still arrest it and bring it back to a solid and save his silver. He also told us of visiting a mine where the chemical processes in the great laboratory of nature were still being carried on, and the silver was forming from a gaseous state.

So we trace matter beyond our present power of vision. How many states and conditions beyond the gaseous before it reaches the spiritual we know not, but we know that somewhere in the unseen and the unseeable is its original and eternal state. For God helps us on this point when he says "The things that are seen are temporal, but the things that are unseen are eternal." We believe that we shall yet find that spirit is the only *true* substance, the original substance from which all substance has originated. The spirit world is the world of causes and this is the world of effects.

Dr. Wilford Hall, of New York, whose scientific works mark an era in the history of science greater than the discoveries of any scientist of this age, or, perhaps we can say, of any other age, has had the boldness to proclaim the doctrine, that all things, whether matter or mind, emanated from God's spiritual essence, and he has brought down the vengeance of two worlds —the scientific and theological—upon his head, but I believe he will, Sampson-like, slay them hip and thigh. He perhaps is not substantially correct in all things. He does not claim infallibility, but he has done more for true science and revelation than any man of the present day. Noble man, may God's blessing be upon him!

It was not necessary that we should trace matter back to its origin for our purposes here; nor as far back as Bishop Warren takes it, to its spirit origin. He says, "Into what more ethereal, and we might almost say, spiritual forms, matter may be changed we cannot tell." And again he says, "We ask in vain What is matter? No man can answer. We trace it up through the worlds till its increasing fineness, its growing power and possible identity of substance seem as if the next step would reveal its spirit origin," and he evidently holds that God's word teaches it, for he adds, "What we but *hesitatingly* stammer the word *boldly* asserts." And Joseph Cook, in his 156th Monday lecture, says, "Look first at the fact that matter originated in the unseen universe. Scientific theism has always had a right, but in our age it has a new right to assert this unflinchingly in the face of atheism, agnosticism and materialism." Again, " The law of continuity requires us to go back step by step from subsequent to antecedent, so that, when we reach the organization of atoms, and of their groupings and motions, we come at last to the unseen universe, to the substance of absolute and infinite being, to the mind and will of the omnipresent God. Having traced back matter to the unseen universe, let us now trace back natural life to the same source." And again he says, in lecture No. 168, March 10th, 1884, " Lotze taught that, from the idea of matter, life and soul cannot be explained; but that, from the idea of spirit all material properties may be deduced." He makes spirit the ultimate substance of all things.

The supersensible reality underlying both matter and finite mind is God.   *   *   *   "Through the English and Scottish philosophy have led you up, little by little, under different circumstances, to the unseen universe. In it we have found the origin of matter, motion and life."

But we will not go as far back as this; we will take it in the gaseous state, then you can adopt the nebula hypothesis, or any hypothesis you may chose except the *pure* evolution theory.

Somewhere back of a gaseous condition, was the chaotic state, must have been, as all material substances take the globular form when suspended in space; the raindrop conforms to this principle, or law.

The planets when formed are found in a state of incandescence, but the tendency in everything in space is to cool. After long periods of cooling they form a solid crust on the surface. The cooling goes on until the crust is thick enough to support vegetation, the lowest forms first, the planet now begins to attain to a life period, or in other words, is becoming capable of sustaining life. It will eventually pass beyond its life period. Our moon is an illustration of it; it has become an opaque body—cold and frigid. Jupiter has not attained to its life period. It is in a state of incandescence, and astronomers estimate that it will take many millions of years of cooling to form a crust upon its surface, then the cooling will progress much slower until it reached its life-sustaining condition. Beautiful venus is doubtless just emerging into its life period. It has water and an atmosphere, and many things very similar to our planet earth.

The planet called earth upon which we live was the first to attain to a life period. And this proposition leads us into theology again. Here God commenced the stupendous plan of peopling the planets, and consequently here he placed that new order of beings, before unknown in his moral universe, spiritual, moral beings united to a material body to capacitate them for living in a material world. And in this new order of beings is found that connecting link between the material and spiritual world, that profound mystery of mysteries, the union of spirit and matter. Man is the desideratum of the universe, he fills the wide gap between the seen and the unseen. He was placed here a pure, holy and happy being, perfectly happy because perfectly holy. He was placed here in a state of probation and had the federal head of the race stood their probation, each individual member of the race as they ended their probation would have been translated from this sphere something in the manner that Enoch and Elijah were, though their translation was a type of something else brought out farther on in these papers. The scripture never types anything in the past, all their figures and types find their antetypes in the future.

But the evil influence that had crept into God's moral government sometime in the past, approached these happy beings, the latest of God's intelligent creation, and accomplished their fall. Now there has been much speculation about the fall of our first parents, and much very irreverent speculation even outspoken censuring of God for creating a pair that he knew would fall and bring so much sorrow and suffering into the world. But it did not matter with God's plans whether they stood or fell. God knew what he would do in either case. If they had endured their probation Satan would have applied his temptations to each individual member of the race the same as he does now, and when he had secured ones fall, they would have fallen without remedy for there would have been no Savior provided in that case, so Satan would have won over as many souls in one case as in the other, there would have been no difference in that respect. But as for me, I thank God that the case is as it now is, for now if I fall a hundred times in a day I can look up to a blessed Savior and rise again. That this was the first planet God peopled with this new order of beings stands to reason. The Devil was already in the battle field and would be sure to assault the first created, knowing that that whole order of beings were secured if he secured the representative head. The vain talk of some people about the Savior dying for other worlds and people, as though the Devil waited until God had peopled a great number of the planets and then started on a very successful tour, kicking over what the Lord had done, and reaching this planet when there was but two on it and found a very easy conquest, and,—according to their theory—the blessed Savior has been going from world to world, for perhaps millions of years, passing through the awful suffering and death for fallen beings, following up the trail of the old Serpent. This seems too silly, yea, too God dishonoring to need refutation.

Nay, fallen Lucifer dealt his severest blow against God's moral government in the earthly Paradise. We cannot think that the Devil ever hoped to overreach infinite wisdom, or overthrow God's plans, he knew that was impossible for any being to do, but he was instigated then, as now, by his totally depraved heart to do all the evil he can to God's creatures and to God's moral government, but God has so overruled it, and made the wrath of devils, as well as "the wrath of men to praise him," that all that hell has done against him shall only help him to consummate his plans and secure his government on a firmer foundation.

God says he will get this evil out of His moral government and confine it to its own place, where "it shall not hurt nor destroy in all His holy mountain" (holy government); mountain in the prophecies means government. And he will yet accomplish his purposes with the human race and the material worlds of his universe. He will yet people the planets and people them, too, with loyal subjects, holy, happy beings, as he intended at the first. He will not have any more such scenes enacted as has been enacted on this planet. It used to be a mystery with us why God could not people a world without it resulting in such a ruinous state of things as we behold here, and why he should suffer a race of intelligent beings to exist one day where there is so much suffering and sorrow and affliction, so much injustice and oppression, etc., if His plans were circumscribed to the narrow limits of this little planet. But God's plans are as broad as the universe.

We used to think that the Scriptures used extravagant language. When God started his kingdom in the world in the form of the little Hebrew republic and church in the land of Canaan, he promised to increase them until they could not be numbered. He said they should be "as the stars of the sky in multitude, and as the sand which is by the seashore, innumerable." The jews understood these promises to apply to carnal Israel, the Hebrew Church and State, but they were intended for Christian Israel, when the spiritual seed of Abraham should not only possess the world, but *worlds*.

There never was a time when carnal Israel could not be

numbered, and when Christian Israel shall possess the whole world—which is unequivocally promised—we presume the census of the world can then be taken. And yet there will be a time when God's Israel will be beyond the computation of finite minds. When God first organized His people in the wilderness if you had stood upon mount Peor with Balaam you would have seen Israel camped in the valley of Moab, 3,000,000 of souls, and as you beheld God's presence with them in the majestic pillar of cloud upon the tabernacle, you might have been made to exclaim with Balaam in the sublime language, "How goodly are thy tents, O Jacob, and thy tabernacles, O Israel. * * * The Lord, his God is with him, and the shout of a king is among them." Again, when Christ sits at the head of the millennial kingdom and rules the world, if you could be raised to some angel tower, and like Jesus on the Mount of Temptation, behold all the kingdoms of the world, you would behold many hundred millions; but when the "desire of all nations" has come and brought with him the perfection of God's kingdom on earth, and God's people like the pure angelic spirits shall have the privilege of God's universe, then look at the lights that adorn the hill of heaven at night, and behold Israel's camp-fires.

Perhaps before we close we should say something about the doctrine of the destructionists. Those who think they see it taught in revelation that our planet is to be annihilated, and talk very eloquently about the "wreck of matter and the crash of worlds." But perhaps I can't answer this strange doctrine more effectually in the same space than to quote from Dr. Baldwin. He says, in commenting on the following Scripture, as follows: "The earth and heaven fled away; and I saw a new heaven and a new earth, for the first heaven and the first earth were passed away, and there was no more sea." This is literal, because the term sea, in the connection in which it stands, cannot be made to receive a symbolic sense. This was the long promised regeneration of the globe. Some severe destructionists have been advocates of the total annihilation of the globe, from a strange misconception of the meaning of this, and other passages of Scripture; but no theory can be more destitute of truth and good sense. The truth is, the destruction of the present heaven and earth is necessary to accomplish the promise of the full glory of God, by preparing the globe for the erection of the throne of David and of God upon it forever. We will briefly meet the theory on its merits. It is affirmed that the heaven and earth that are to be destroyed, signify the globe This we deny most positively.

1. The term earth has at least twelve significations, and the term world has twenty-two Now, it is not by any means necessary to give the signification of globe, to the term earth; whenever it is used, and especially when the context does not require it.

2. The term heaven and earth is used by Moses, and most certainly do not signify the globe; for he expressly defines them to signify only parts of the mundane system. Thus, he says, "God called the *dry land* earth, and God called the *firmament* (or atmosphere) heaven," "and the *gathering together* of water called the seas." Here is as clear a definition of these terms, by inspiration itself, as could be desired. Now, as it is illogical and falsifying to give the terms of an author a different sense from that which he has expressly given them so it is falsifying God's word to insist that he means the destruction of the globe, when he speaks of the destruction of heaven and earth, and sea, which he had defined to be but exterior parts of the globe.

3 St. Peter, who gives a description of the heavens and earth, literally by fire, teaches plainly that he does not mean a destruction of the globe, but only a renewal of it by fire; and Moses in his description of the destruction of the earth by the deluge, concurs with our views. Thus, he says, "I will destroy

them with the earth;" "a flood to destroy the earth." Peter says: "By the word of God, the heavens were of old, and the earth standing out of the water, and in the water, whereby the world that then was, being overflowed with water, perished; but the heavens and earth which are now, by the same word, are kept in store, reserved unto fire against the day of judgment." Nothing can be plainer than that the old heavens and earth before the flood, perished, and that the globe did not; and nothing can be plainer than, "that the heavens and earth which are now," are as much different from the globe as were the heavens and earth before the flood. It is as clear as light, that the heavens and earth destroyed by water have the same signification as the term heaven and earth, which are to be destroyed by fire. So that the destruction announced by Peter has no sort of reference to a destruction of the globe, but only to its external organization. Besides, he says, "according to his promise, we look for new heavens and a new earth."

Now, the only special promise upon this subject, was given by Isaiah, and he locates them upon the present globe. It therefore follows, that when Christ said, "the heaven and earth shall pass away," he referred to the present heaven and earth, erected upon the globe, and not the globe itself.

4. "The reason for the passing away of the heaven and earth. There is good sense in every act of God, and hence there is a good common sense reason for the destruction of the present heaven and earth, and that reason is as obvious as it is sensible; it is to restore the world to its pristine glory. The war which God declared in the beginning, was for the conquest of the world; to restore man upon earth to subjection to his government. Now, the curse upon the ground was a great act of war, to aid in the subjugation of the race; and the curse on the earth was a double one; the first at the Fall and the second by the Flood. After the conquest of man, this curse would, according to the promise at the beginning, be removed; and

this removal would require as great a change in the heaven and earth, at such renewal, as took place when they were changed at the Fall and the Flood; that is, to remove the curse, the heaven and earth would need to be removed or changed. The promise of the final removal of the curse, on all things, was made at the first, and repeated in all subsequent ages. The removal of the curse of death implies a resurrection; and the removal of the curse on the heavens and earth, implies their removal, and the erection of a heaven and earth without imper fection, and not the annihilation of the globe, which would be the severest punishment ever inflicted on it.

5. The annihilation of the globe implies that God entertains spite against inanimate matter, which is most absurd to suppose.

6. God has engaged in war for six thousand years, to establish his kingdom on the globe. Now, what good sense is there in fighting for ages, through the most awful scenes of affliction, to regain a revolted province on purpose to annihilate it as soon as it is possessed? Tell us, ye wise! Say, is there reason in the baseless assumption you make? God swore to Moses that the whole earth should be full of his glory; and the prophets say that it shall then endure forever. Does this look like annihilation of the globe? Does it not look like its regeneration at the final "restitution of all things?"

7. John says, that after the old heaven and earth were gone, that the New Jerusalem descended to the new earth, and to the region where the curse had prevailed. The words, "there shall be no more death, neither shall there be any more pain; for the former things are passed away," are applicable to a world where these things had prevailed, and from which they were banished, and not to a world where they had never been known. "Behold, I make all things new," can not refer to the third heaven, but only to a world where every thing needed reorganization. "There shall be no more curse," applies only

to a world where the curse had prevailed. But, again: All these things were prophecies, to be fulfilled after the days of John, and they must refer to this globe, and not to the third heaven, which existed before John's day. Besides this, the New Jerusalem came down from God, out of heaven, to men, and men did not go up to it; which shows, again, that this globe was to be the throne of God and the Lamb. Daniel, and Isaiah, and all the prophets, make the world redeemed to abide forever; and after the millennium is ended, and the judgment is passed, John shows the state of the world in the full blaze of celestial glory. Who ever heard of Christ's returning from the earth after his second advent to it? And who has not read that the tabernacle of God shall be with men after the New Jerusalem descends, and that they shall reign with God and the Lamb forever and ever in the New Jerusalem, and in the heavens and earth, from which the curse had been removed? The truth is, the regenerated globe is to be the battle monument of eternity; the seat of government of Jesus, head over all things; the holy of holies of the universe. As the believers shall come from the dust, where the curse had laid them, and shall wear the image of Jesus, and shall be adorned with all the glory which infinite skill can compass, or Omnipotence create; so also shall their residence, freed from the curse, appear in all the splendor commensurate with its citizens and king. As the throne of the Son of Mary will shine with all the splendors of Deity; as it will be the supreme expression of all the concentrated excellence with which matter can be clothed by Jehovah's limitless resources and power, so this poor blood-stained globe will shine, wrapped in the uncreated blaze of God's robe of royalty; so it will be filled with eternal music and delight; so it will be holy, holy, holy to the Lord God of hosts; so it will be an eternal honor to the Captain of our salvation. When the serpent's head is bruised, when the curse shall fly from earth and hover forever over the lost, in the night of their woe, may you and I, dear reader, have a shelter beneath the jasper skies and trees of life, beside the living streams of joy. Then from our central home, upon Jehovah's wing, O be it ours to visit every home of angels, and know in person every creature of his love, in every world of his own universe, and pass eternity delightfully! This regeneration of the globe completes the victory foretold to the serpent; it is the "kingdom come on earth, as it is in heaven."

In those times what shall limit the privileges of God's people? Shall they not take the swift flying chariots of Jehovah, that have brought angelic spirits and redeemed souls (Moses and Elijah, and others) to our world and carried them away again. Shall they not, I ask, be privileged those lightning trains, and visit worlds basking in all the loveliness that God's perfection of beauty can bestow. It is not too wild a flight of imagination to say you will call some day at those beautiful worlds and enquire,

"Stopped here the good Enoch on his way,
Called here Elijah in his flaming car."

It is not saying too much to say you will some time walk the flowery fields and beautiful groves of lovely Venus; quaff the limpid waters of her youth-giving fountains, or stand beneath Saturn's majestic rings and behold the grandeur of her evening skies, with her eight moons and luminary belts.

It may seem chimerical to some of the scientists of our day to talk about traveling away from our planet, but two have traveled the route before us, Enoch and Elijah, and their translation is the pledge, proof, and pattern of ours. About 1,900 years ago they paid us a visit, and talked awhile with Jesus on the Mount of Transfiguration; spoke of his decease which he should accomplish at Jerusalem, finished their mission and returned to their bright home. They will doubtless never visit us again until Christ comes in his kingdom. Poor old Elisha saw Elijah when he jumped aboard of the fiery train and rode away, and with outstretched arms and anxious heart he cried after him, but alas, his time had not then come for the glorious flight.

Extravagant language, do you say? Imagination can not plume her wing for too high a flight or too broad a sweep when God's plans and promises are her pursuit.

God grant, my dear reader, that we may be counted among God's worthy people who shall one day drop sorrow, care, death and age, and in perennial youth soar to the bright worlds above and around us.

Then go, Christian, go! and with the angels

"Wing thy flight from star to star,"
"From world to luminous world as far"
Taste "all the pleasures of all the spheres,"
Enjoy "them through endless years;"
And then thy heaven has just begun.

www.ingramcontent.com/pod-product-compliance
Lightning Source LLC
Chambersburg PA
CBHW020302090426
42735CB00009B/1181